WORK STRESS

ALAN A. McLEAN, M.D.

IBM Corporation and
Cornell University Medical College

WORK STRESS

ADDISON-WESLEY PUBLISHING COMPANY

Reading, Massachusetts • Menlo Park, California
Don Mills, Ontario • Wokingham, England
Amsterdam • Sydney • Singapore • Tokyo
Mexico City • Bogotá • Santiago • San Juan

WITHDRAWN

This book is the first in the
Addison-Wesley Series on Occupational Stress

Library of Congress Cataloging in Publication Data

McLean, Alan A
    Catalyst for change.

    (Occupational stress series)
    1. Job stress. I. Title. II. Series.
HF5548.85.M3   158.7   78-73370
ISBN 0-201-04592-3

Seventh Printing, July 1985

ISBN 0-201-04592-3
    GHIJK-AL-898765

To each of us who copes daily with work stress

FOREWORD

The vast literature concerned with the individual coping with work
stress stems from many and diverse disciplines, primarily psychiatry,
clinical and social psychology, sociology, cultural anthropology, and
occupational and internal medicine, with significant contributions
from such widely different fields as behavioral toxicology and personnel and management. While each discipline is concerned with so-
called "psychosocial stressors," communication between the several
disciplines has generally been the exception rather than the rule.
Lawyers, for example, tend to communicate mainly with other
lawyers about the issues that concern them. Union leaders tend to
communicate most often with other union leaders. Clinical psychologists direct their communications to their colleagues, but use a different language from that used by many of the psychiatrists who are
equally concerned. Even social psychologists and industrial sociol-
ogists sometimes find it difficult to exchange data. The transfer of useful data from one discipline to another has proven to be very difficult.
"Some researchers go about rediscovering the known, with little defer-
ence to an existing literature or to determinable frontiers for contemporary research; and what consensus may be possible is *not ade-
quately disseminated for beneficial application beyond home base.*"*

---

* Robert Rose, editorial, *Journal of Human Stress,* Vol. 3 No. 1, March
1977.

Communication across disciplines is not the only difficulty that students of job-related stress encounter. Transcultural communication is a problem too. Western physiologists, for instance, who are concerned with hormones in the brain, have difficulty communicating with their eastern European colleagues who prefer to speak in terms of "higher nervous function."

There is growing common concern. Theories and practices in each discipline are beginning to cross-pollinate other disciplines and to exert a positive influence toward understanding the stresses of the workplace and workers' reactions.

The many denominators of concern for an employee population under stress form the unifying theme of these volumes. As a field of study, occupational stress is beginning to gel. It is a subject of increasing interest not only to members of unions and management, but also to the health professionals who serve as their consultants. Increasingly, awareness and expertise are being focused on both theoretical and practical problem solving. The findings of social scientists have led to the enactment of legislation in the Scandinavian countries, for instance, where employers are now required, under certain circumstances, to provide meaningful work and appropriate job satisfaction with a minimum of occupational stress.

The authors of these books represent many points of view and a variety of disciplines. Each, however, is interested in the same basic thing—greater job satisfaction and greater productivity for each employee. The books were written independently with only broad guidelines and coordination by the editor. Each is a unique, professional statement summarizing an area closely related to the main theme. Each extracts from that area applications which seem logically based on currently available knowledge.

All of the authors treat, from differing perspectives, three key concepts: stress, stressor, and stress reactions. *Stress* defines a process or a system which includes not only the stressful event and the reaction to it, but all the intervening steps between. The *stressor* is a stressful event or stressful condition that produces a psychological or physical reaction in the individual that is usually unpleasant and sometimes produces symptoms of emotional or physiological disability. The *stress reaction* concerns the consequences of the stimulus provided by a stressor. It is, in other words, the response to a stressor, and it is generally unhealthy. Most often, such reactions may be defined in rather traditional psychological terms, ranging from mild situational anxiety and depression to serious emotional disability.

Many frames of reference are represented in this series. A psychoanalyst describes the phenomenon of occupational stress in executives. A sociologist reflects the concern with blue-collar workers. Health-care-delivery systems and the prevention of occupational stress reactions are covered by occupational physicians. Other authors focus on social support systems and on physiological aspects of stress reactions. All the authors are equally concerned with the reduction of unhealthy environmental social stimuli both in the world of work and in the other aspects of life that the world of work affects. In each instance, the authors are concerned with defining issues and with drawing the kinds of conclusions that will suggest constructive solutions.

The legal system, beginning with worker's compensation statutes and more recently augmented by the Occupational Safety and Health Act, deals directly with occupational stress reactions and will be the subject of one of the books in the series. That statute, which created both the Occupational Safety and Health Administration and the National Institute for Occupational Safety and Health, contains a specific directive mandating study of psychologically stressful factors in the work environment. We have seen criteria documents and standards for physical factors in the work environment. We may soon see standards developed to govern acceptable levels of psychological stressors at work such as already exist in Sweden and Norway; another significant area of concern for this series.

At the beginning of this series it is difficult to foresee all the pivotal areas of interest which should be covered. It is even more difficult to predict the authors who will be able and willing to confront the issues as they emerge in the next few years. In a rapidly changing technological, scientific, and legislative world, the challenge will be to bring contemporary knowledge about occupational stress to an audience of intelligent managers who can translate thoughts into constructive action.

Alan A. McLean, M.D.
Editor

INTRODUCTION: PERSPECTIVE

Conceptually this book was born in the backyard sun of summer at Martha's Vineyard many years ago. For some time, I had been trying to find a linkage—a framework—upon which to organize the most important variables related to occupational stress. At that point I needed both to identify the variables and to conceive a way of demonstrating their relationship that would be useful to me and meaningful to others—particularly to the decision makers in work organizations, the people through whom positive change is accomplished in the world of work.

I was familiar with many complex models of the relationship between stressful factors at work and resulting symptoms, of feedback models which included a host of intervening variables, of sophisticated psychological and sociological models, often mind boggling in their complexity. But I sought simplicity, dynamism.

It took very little time in Martha's Vineyard's sun to recognize that stressful events and conditions were key variables in the relationship. It seemed reasonable to me finally to organize these many factors into three major categories: individual vulnerability to stressors, the environment in which that vulnerability is exposed to stressors, and the resulting behavioral symptoms (which may be subtle or complex).

Having decided to use stressors, vulnerability, context, and symptoms as the base, I needed a dynamic schemata that would demonstrate the complex interaction of these variables. The one that appears to work best is a simple matrix of at times overlapping circles that represent the variables in question.

In this book I establish a frame of reference in the first two chapters and discuss three of the major variables of job stress in the next four chapters. Then, in the concluding three chapters, I treat methods of preventing stress reaction, coping with it when it crops up, and assessing the degree to which stressors on the job can be disturbing.

My personal perspective has been shaped by my years as a physician. It has been quite logical for me to draw heavily on the medical model—a model which requires objectively assessing all relevant evidence, considering a series of alternative possible conclusions, selecting the most logical, confirming the diagnosis, and, finally, instituting a treatment program.

In dealing with occupational stress, one does not evaluate an individual's job status—his or her reaction to an occupational situation—simply on the basis of research studies of *many* test subjects. Nor can one base such an evaluation on averages, norms, means, or medians of groups of persons exposed to seemingly similar events. Rather, at issue is usually a single individual and a single evaluator (physician, psychiatrist, psychologist, manager). Each is accustomed to playing a professional role. Each is influenced by his or her role. Each evaluates a potentially stressful situation according to his or her training, background, and, often, personality makeup.

In one sense, such an assessment becomes a test of perceptiveness. Hopefully, the professional can be objective, encompassing, and honest and render a useful opinion or suggestion in the best interests of both the individual and the organization. This process of diagnosis is often exceedingly complicated, involving a careful evaluation of a single individual at a specific point in time and in a particular job. There are well-established, deeply ingrained, and systematic techniques which have been practiced by generations of clinicians, mainly physicians. It is this complex system of diagnosis and treatment of the individual patient that is the perspective of this volume. And my concern is with the prospective patient—the employee at risk.

Nevertheless, this is not a book about psychiatric illness as a reaction to job stress. The fact that I have used a few such case illustrations should not mislead the reader. Extreme reactions are sometimes part of a stress reaction and have been included for that reason. But my main focus is on the essentially healthy person reacting to the daily events and conditions of his or her work.

ACKNOWLEDGMENTS

In the two years gestation of the Occupational Stress series and this, the introductory volume, dozens of colleagues and friends made valuable suggestions, offered constructive criticism, and worked over all or parts of the manuscript. While I assume total responsibility for the contents of this volume, I would like to acknowledge particularly the work of other series authors: Lennart Levi, Leonard Moss, Arthur Shostak, and Leon Warshaw. Since a project like this is perforce a family affair, my thanks and special affection go to my wife, Jan, my sons, Dick and Bob, and to both my parents, Elizabeth and Winfield, each of whom in a uniquely special way contributed significantly. Others deserving of more than passing gratitude include David Bertelli, Roger Brach, Pat Carrington and Barrie Greiff. The editorial efforts of Norman Stanton, Charles T. Peers, Jr., and Barbara Pendergast at Addison-Wesley added immeasurably to the quality of the final product. Besides that, they were fun to work with! Finally the enormous contributions of two wonderfully competent and patient secretaries, Eleanor Kirchmer and Dorothy Diamond, helped make the writing task stimulating rather than stressful.

Westport, Connecticut   A.A.M.
February 1979

CONTENTS

1

THE STRESS
OF WORK

Work occupies a major part of most of our lives, in terms of both time spent and importance. It contains the *potential* for many forms of gratification and challenge—and harm. It is not surprising that a great many of us at times find work life stressful. Indeed, stress at work is so commonplace that we tend to accept it as part of the necessary frustration of daily living. The abrasive boss, the boredom and monotony of an assembly operation, the new processes that demand skills we do not seem to have, the threat of job loss: Many stressors are simply annoying; a few lead to serious disability; some actually cause death. This chapter includes examples of a variety of such cases, and I will comment briefly on each to introduce the more severe forms of stress reaction.

Consider a personal example. Several years ago I was returning to my then home in Lexington, Kentucky, from a New York business trip. The plane descended to the Lexington airport but a few feet off the runway, with a roar of seemingly urgent acceleration and a surge of power, it pulled up sharply. We circled the field several times. I could clearly see my family waiting below. In a few minutes there was a terse announcement from the pilot, "The landing gear won't go down!" The two stewardesses disappeared into the cockpit. For the next hour and a half there was no further communication from the flight deck and no sign of the stewardesses. We approached Louisville and circled the field innumerable times with several passes just a few hundred feet above the tower. We could see the fire apparatus lined up along the runway. No further word from the flight deck; no sign of the stewardesses; no response to the many stewardess call buttons which were alight. The seat belt sign and no smoking sign had remained on since prior to the approach in Lexington. The level of fear and apprehension in the cabin was heightened further as we made a final approach to the runway with one engine sputtering. The landing was uneventful.

In questioning the captain afterwards, I was told that an indicator light had malfunctioned and that it had been necessary to obtain visual verification that the nose wheel was in place before attempting a landing. I asked him why he had not informed the passengers and why the stewardesses had remained up front with him. He seemed perplexed and nonplussed that this behavior would be upsetting; it had not occurred to him that passengers had any need or right to know what was going on, what his plans were, and what their degree of jeopardy might be.

In times of stress, management must *be* there. The presence of authority figures who are available both to answer questions and to *lead* is essential. Great assurance and reassurance can be drawn from the simple presence of those in command. Dependency needs in times of stress are heightened and a demonstration that one's superior cares and recognizes the impact of stress on the employee under his or her supervision will reap incalculable rewards.

The following case illustrates even better the impact of stressors. I first heard about this case more than twenty-five years ago from a colleague who was studying the operation of a paper-manufacturing plant. The circumstances are tragic, but the case is a perfect example of vulnerability to occupational stress reaction. The patient, a paper cutter about sixty years old who had a long history of successful experience in a large manufacturing plant, began complaining of headaches. He consulted his private physician and the plant's physician and both confirmed that he had developed moderately severe high blood pressure. His knowledge of this condition increased his vulnerability and made him more anxious. Then one day, he fainted just after getting out of bed in the morning. This worried him further. Both his physician and the doctor at the plant advised that he seek an early retirement since there was increased likelihood that he might experience an accident on the job. A very favorable pension plan was arranged. Nonetheless he had great misgivings. His friends were almost exclusively his coworkers. His job was the major part of his life. With a great deal of ambivalence, much hesitation, and considerable anxiety, he accepted his company's offer even though he felt he would be lost without work. His last day on the job came. During the three final hours at his machine, despite all safeguards, he cut off his right hand. This was his first accident on the job.

The relationship between major vulnerability—such as the paper cutter's despair at losing his job—and accidents is clear: This accident was a symptom and a consequence of stress. Yet even in this case, which stemmed from such an obvious psychological foundation, it was almost impossible to predict such an outcome. No one could have predicted the failure of carefully designed safeguards against such an accident. But one *can* recognize that almost any engineering devices designed to prevent accidents can be bested by those who are intimately aware of their workings. With twenty-twenty hindsight, the paper cutter *should* have been removed from his job immediately once the decision had been made that he was a potential threat to himself or others. A desk job for the last few weeks at work may not have guaranteed against an accident, but it would have reduced the potential. Often we fail to act when someone's vulnerability soars and a potentially hazardous environment remains unchanged.

Stress reactions of a symptomatic nature are not always as transient or readily attributable to temporary insecurity. Symptoms could be produced as well by an overwhelming stressor or by the rapid modification of a supporting context.

STRESS AND WORK

There has been a tremendous amount of research into the so-called stress of work, particularly that associated with what we may think of as the psychosocial aspects of work. This information is scattered and uneven and has not been assembled in a useful way for the person who most needs to understand it—the executive responsible for the operations of work organizations, the individual who may be held accountable for stressful work environments.

The research shows the relationship between stressors on the job and physical and emotional changes in individuals. Perhaps the most compelling studies demonstrate that psychological stressors produce altered measurements of various bodily chemicals, hormones, and organic functions as well as altered levels of anxiety. And this happens both in real-life work situations and in the laboratory. We also know that changes at work bring about needs to adjust which, in turn, stimulate reactions, some of which may be unhealthy.

Responses to stressful situations at work have been measured by psychological self-ratings, performance appraisals, and biochemical tests as well as the usual clinical studies of employees presenting symptoms. In a series of such studies, Lennart Levi (Head of the World Health Organization Research Center on Psychosocial Factors and Health) and Bertil Gardell (Associate Professor of Work Psychology at the University of Stockholm) have demonstrated the manner in which stimuli at work affect physical reactions in a potentially damaging manner.

In an experiment lasting seventy-five hours, Levi studied thirty-two senior military officers who alternated between three-hour sessions on an electronic shooting range and performing military staff work. Such a regimen of both psychomotor and intellectual tasks is present in many civilian occupations as well. No relaxation or sleep was allowed, nor were stimulants, smoking, or walking. Although the emotional reactions thus provoked were of only moderate intensity, significant biochemical changes in components of the blood were found to occur at the end of the test period indicating increased anxiety (Levi, 1974).

A study by Gardell illustrates the adverse effects on workers of poor design of the work process. The subjects of his study included one risk group and two age-matched control groups. The members of risk group were skilled workers completing a series of operations within a time period of less than ten seconds. The workers could not talk to their colleagues because of the noise and the need for constant attention, nor could they leave their operating area without special permission. The control group had greater variety, freedom, and self-control in performing their jobs.

The group at risk reported that they had much higher job dissatisfaction and anxiety; they also had higher levels of boredom, "mental strain," and social isolation. In addition, they had a general tendency toward more sick leave and complaints, and they expressed the feeling that their ill health was due to the constraints of their jobs.

At the conclusion of a work shift, studies of adrenaline secretion demonstrated a high level of arousal in the risk group, which suggests that it took several hours of relaxation after work before normal bodily levels were reached (Gardell, 1975).

There is also quite convincing work demonstrating the relationship between occupational factors and coronary heart disease, hypertension, and ulcers. Further, the relationship between various occupational roles and increased incidence of a variety of psychosomatic disorders is clear. We know that significant life changes seem to occur just prior to major disability—and that many of these changes are occupationally related. (See Chapter 5.)

John French and Robert Caplan at the University of Michigan in 1972 noted that work overload correlates with job-related threat. They tested and proved the hypothesis that overload is associated with increases in both cholesterol level and heart rate.

The same authors evaluated the stressfulness of role ambiguity. Men who suffered ambiguity in their work experienced lower job satisfaction and higher job-related tensions. They conclude that role ambiguity was significantly related to job-related threats to mental and physical well-being.

In several studies, the Michigan group has shown that a variety of forms of work overload produce at least nine different kinds of psychological and physiological signs of strain in the worker. Four of these (job dissatisfaction, elevated cholesterol, elevated heart rate, and smoking) are risk factors in heart disease. They conclude that reducing work overload will reduce heart disease.

An intriguing piece of research which clearly illustrates the relationship of overload, underload, and stress was published in the February 1977 issue of the *Journal of Occupational Medicine*. Clinton Weiman at Cornell University Medical College correlated perceived occupational stressors with disease and/or the risk of disease. He studied 1,540 officers of a major company who underwent voluntary periodic health examinations, including the administration of a questionnaire which contained items about occupational stressors. Those executives in the low *and* high ends of the stress-score ranges scored significantly higher in measures of meaningful medical problems, confirming the hypothesis that the relationship between stressors and disease is curvilinear. Weiman's data seems to demonstrate that those who are bored or understimulated and those who feel highly pressured represent the two ends of a continuum, each with a significantly elevated number of symptoms.

It therefore seems clear that there exists fairly rigorous research data to support the relationship between various occupations and psychological disorder. Much more will be described in the next several chapters, but it is important to recognize at the beginning that our subject has been well researched in many areas—these conclusions and judgments do not come out of thin air. Some observations build from research; others from clinical cases and medical experience.

The following case brings out some of the more subtle work influences that affect how a person may react to seemingly minor stressors in the surrounding environment.

The patient, a thirty-two year old man who works as a free-lance writer, was referred to a psychiatrist because of headaches and back and abdominal pain. Several physical examinations, specialty consultations, and laboratory studies revealed no organic basis for his symptoms. Yet he was clearly disabled. The discomfort was obvious as he moved slowly, sank guardedly into his chair, and sat rigidly during an interview.

Important in this patient's developmental history was the fact that he had been raised by an elderly mother whose two older, unmarried sisters also lived in the home. He was the only child. He never knew his father. In effect, he was raised by three mothers, and from the beginning they expected him to adhere to their adult and feminine standards. He was never, for instance, allowed to express his anger directly.

As he moved through high school and college, he was a social isolate, but he did well in school and, from an early age, demonstrated a literary talent, which he subsequently exploited in a variety of writing assignments. He found that he was uncomfortable working in a socially demanding environment, first as a wire-service copy boy, later as a journalist. He was able to make a reasonably good living in an independent capacity—some years doing quite well, others marginally. But this depended on commissions and royalties, which varied with his productivity—productivity which was at times limited by disabling psychosomatic symptoms.

At age twenty-eight he married a woman much like his mother and her sisters. She also was a writer but demonstrated more talent than he and consistently brought in more money. It soon became clear that his pain was more severe when his wife did especially well. The first time she received a large advance for a book, he was disabled for three weeks.

Our culture places a great deal of emphasis upon success. It also teaches us that physical illness is acceptable; mental illness is not. Our patient was clearly the sort who could not express his anger and frustration at his wife's success through any direct route or through overt emotional illness. Yet his pain was real. Here is a rather classic situational illness which can be understood in the context of the psychological realities engendered by early developmental influences and the changing context represented by his wife's changing career. Here, too, is an early suggestion of the complexity of many stress reactions and of the origins of some psychiatric symptoms. It also gives a hint of the excitement and challenge involved in trying to understand the reasons why people react as they do to specific stressors.

JOB STRESS AND WORKER COMPENSATION

As one might expect, there are enormous legal ramifications in the job-stress equation. An employer generally is liable for disability that stems from the work setting. In addition, there are no assurances against liability for physical or emotional symptoms that are mainly the result of particular and unique vulnerabilities of the employee. (I am not suggesting there should be.)

Worker compensation laws now make an employer legally liable for an employee's mental illness, whatever its deep-seated or underlying cause, if it is aggravated, accelerated, precipitated, or triggered to the point of disability or need for medical care by any condition of the employment. This is true regardless of whether the employee himself or herself produced or participated in the production of the conditions of employment that may have operated as precipitating, aggravating or accelerating factors. Fault or absence from fault on the part of either the employer or the employee plays no part whatsoever in determining the liability of the employer for the payment of worker compensation benefits or the entitlement of the employee to receive such benefits (Lesser, 1967).

Consider the following. The Christmas season always made John Gorman, security director of a Rochester, New York, department store, tense and nervous. Usually he calmed down by January, but in January 1971 his anxiety and depression deepened. When a colleague was fired, Mr. Gorman became more withdrawn.

His twenty-seven year old secretary, Diana Wolfe, was close to him, protected him, and shouldered some of his responsibilities. But this time she was unable to cheer him up. On June 9 Mr. Gorman came to the office as usual. A few minutes later, he telephoned Mrs. Wolfe and told her to send the police to his office one floor away. She did, then rushed there herself. She found him lying dead in a pool of blood, the result of a self-inflicted gunshot wound in the head.

The shock of the experience contributed to a serious depression. Mrs. Wolfe was unable to work. She lost twenty pounds. She spent hours in bed staring at the ceiling, silent and withdrawn. She was hospitalized twice, eventually receiving electroshock therapy which finally eased her depression.

Mrs. Wolfe also left her mark on the field of occupational stress. She recovered after a year but still faced $20,000 worth of hospital bills. Her insurance company would not pay and she was told that Worker Compensation did not cover mental illness in New York State. She went to court, however, and finally, in May 1975, she won: the New York Court of Appeals ordered her hospital bills paid by Worker Compensation, ruling that crippling mental illness is as real in the eyes of the law as physical injuries and illnesses.

It was a major victory in New York State, particularly since the court had rejected two earlier job-stress claims. And the ruling resounded throughout the country. Thomas Lambert, editor of the *American Trial Lawyers Association Journal* and a specialist in worker compensation, said that it was a very significant ruling: "The New York Court of Appeals is a prestige-laden court, a bellwether court" whose decisions other states' courts weigh carefully. At least eleven other states and the District of Columbia also award worker compensation for mental and emotional disability resulting from job stress.

Worker compensation is a system that exists by virtue of statutes in states and other jurisdictions to provide medical expenses and a weekly benefit for disabilities that arise from industrial accidents. Increasingly, we have seen mental illness held as compensable. Increasingly, no physical injury is required to meet the definition of an accident. Held as compensable, for instance, have been emotional disability caused by physical trauma, physical disability caused by emotional stress, and emotional disability caused by emotional stressors.

The case that stimulated much of our current interest in this particular area was decided by the Michigan Supreme Court in December 1960. In a five-to-three decision, the court sustained an order of the workmen's compensation appeal board awarding compensation to an employee for a psychotic illness said to have resulted from the emotional pressure he experienced in his daily work as a machine operator on an assembly line. The court held that the continuous criticism of the employee by his foreman *caused* his schizophrenic condition.

A more recent case is *Butler vs. the District Parking Management Company* in the District of Columbia. Mr. Butler worked for the company for twenty years and appeared to be healthy. One day he left the job and did not return; he was hospitalized with a mental disorder. He and his attorney claimed that the "pressures of the job" caused his disability. The court indicated that because the company was unable to disprove this causal relationship, the workmen's compensation benefits were applicable and appropriate. Most workmen's compensation statutes have a section similar to that in the act of the District of Columbia. It says that, in the absence of substantial evidence to the contrary, a given claim does come within the provision of the act. It is not unreasonable to assume that this practice will become universal in the near future, requiring all employers to disprove a causal relationship between the employment and the disability.

I am not concerned about worker compensation as such; I am concerned about many of the disability benefits involved in permanent disability and in sickness and accident-insurance plans. Part of my concern has to do with the difference between the legal and medical definitions of the word "cause."

Physicians consider "cause" as the many underlying factors that lead to the pathology of any illness. Legally, "cause" refers to a factor that contributes to the production of the disability, whether it triggers, aggravates, or renders symptomatic an underlying condition. There is, I think, a very real danger in liberalizing the legal concept of "cause" to the point where anyone can successfully claim that regularly expected performance on the job "causes" mental disorder. In medicine *cause* or "etiology" is much more complex. When a man dislikes his foreman and becomes anxious in his presence, the feeling may well have its roots in that individual's early relationship with authority figures. The individual may consciously believe that the fault lies with the foreman and may stay away from work pleading nervousness and seek compensation. If the compensation courts confirm this type of thinking, they will seriously impede the process of treating the individual. They will tend to reinforce the patient's superficial explanation of the cause of his or her anxiety and interfere with the development of accurate understanding of the *real* reasons for the disability. If the courts ignore cause in the medical sense and pay the employee for believing that disability is based on a single stressor at work, they do the employee a disservice. The implications of such decisions are obviously important to management and clinical practice as well as the employee-patient.

Thus far, the number of cases with disability the apparent result of psychosocial stressors on the job is relatively small. I do not see this as a major problem at the moment, but I do see it as a *potential* one, in part because of the growing concern about job stress.

Rx

This book is not primarily concerned with intervention strategies in cases of people reacting to occupational stressors with serious symptoms of emotional illness. In the last three chapters I will discuss ways in which the organization can reduce the number of stressors an employee must face and suggest coping techniques that may prove helpful in forestalling serious stress reactions, but dealing with serious disability is more than I want to address here. Nevertheless, it is important to do more than simply acknowledge the existence of professional help. Perhaps the next two cases will, by example, illustrate the point.

Case number 1. The case of a forty-three-year-old industrial scientist illustrates one fairly typical stress reaction. He had recently assumed an administrative post calling for the coordination of research endeavors for several scientific groups. In effect, he moved from direct participation in research projects to what he termed "paper pushing." The management of his laboratory saw it as a major promotion. The patient saw it as a waste of his talent and as particularly stressful. He sought a discussion with a psychiatrist as part of his efforts to decide whether it might be best to return to his former position. During the first of three interviews he appeared moderately depressed. His speech was slow, as was his thought.

"I have always had a driving compulsion to do a good job," he said. "I've been fairly successful in basic research and in working with small groups of people. I guess that's why I've been given more and more responsibility. But along with it I've spent almost every night, including weekends, at work. I am the sort of guy who has to be on top of everything and, up to a point, this has been fine. I guess I really wanted this last promotion. I thought I could handle it, though I found several big projects underway with which I was totally unfamiliar. I can't be expected to make intelligent decisions concerning scientific areas in which I've had no experience."

With psychotherapy and antidepressant medication, he rapidly recovered from his depression and was able to do a more effective job coordinating the activity of others. Stemming from his initial feelings of inadequacy in the job, the feelings of depression themselves had interfered with his ability to apply himself to his new assignment. He was soon able to perform satisfactorily in his new job.

As it turned out, this timely psychiatric assistance supported him during a crucial period of his career and, by helping him to gain a clearer picture of his own abilities, contributed both to his own health and to the goals of his laboratory.

Case number 2. A forty-two-year-old manager was conscientious and hard working but very prone to worry. For many years he had been in a job that stretched him to his limit. This was acceptable to him, and his relationship with his superior was very satisfactory. He received only minimal supervision, but his boss was available whenever a real need arose. He experienced full work satisfaction and a sense of well-being. For business reasons, he was transferred to similar work in another department. There his new manager constantly checked his work, seriously reducing his discretionary responsibility. Using his capacity for judgment and decision making fully had been a major element in his work satisfaction; it was the loss in middle age of his discretionary responsibility that he felt most keenly, experiencing it as a major deprivation. His relationship with his new manager deteriorated rapidly and he began to feel strained and to sleep badly, often waking during the early morning hours. He later became more seriously depressed.

He sought the advice of his employer's medical director, who, rather than referring him to a psychiatrist or clinical psychologist, intervened directly with the responsible top management of the division of the company in which he worked. Without anyone the wiser as to the reason, he soon received an invitation to join the staff of another department which needed his particular skills—and that was managed by a man whose style was to delegate authority to a great extent. On the new job his depression lifted rapidly. His productivity rose and the matter was resolved.

Adjustment reactions to changes in supervision are not at all unusual. There is, first, very real and natural apprehension about a new boss. What's he or she like? Will he let me do my thing in the same way? Will she get me the raise that's due? But more than that, different administrative styles stir up different kinds of unconscious conflicts in each member of the work group. A new supervisor must clearly appreciate that he or she will be perceived at two levels: first, at a rational, conscious level on the basis of management skills; and, second, on the basis of how each member of the work group has perceived authority figures over the course of his or her lifetime.

THE CHANGING WORK SCENE

There is a common denominator to most occupational stress, and that is *change*. All change involves loss of some kind. Promotions, demotions, and job transfers, however desired, are examples of changes that result in a loss of familiar faces, places, pleasures, ways of doing things, or organizational supports. And one of the greatest changes to which we all must adapt is the changing nature of work. This in itself is a significant stressor.

To conclude this first chapter, I would set the stage for the balance of the book (and the following volumes in this series) by briefly looking at work and its meaning to the individual and the changes that meaning has undergone in recent years.

MEANING OF WORK

Work has different meaning for the industrial employee at a fixed station on the assembly line, the clerk, the engineer, and the manager. Yet each, in time, experiences change. The rapid change in the meaning of work during these past years is a factor of major importance. Workers increasingly expect work to provide satisfaction and the scientists are increasingly challenged to translate their professional findings into applied knowledge. Much of this change stems from the fact that the work force in Western society is both better educated and more affluent than in prior generations. Workers generally realize that society, for the most part, will not let them starve. There are increasing numbers of nonwork roles that can be assumed, such as welfare dependency, prolonged education, and early retirement. Other nonwork roles with which we are all familiar are absenteeism and disability. It is common for somone to become disabled and to find that, consciously or unconsciously, he or she derives great satisfaction from the dependent state, finding little motivation to return to a monotonous routine.

A few years ago the values and ethics of American youth began to permeate the work force, and younger workers brought new perspectives. In routine assignments they had considerable difficulty in adjusting and, for a time, they continued to be restless, mobile, changeable, and demanding. In the automobile industry, one-third of the employees are age thirty or younger. In the early seventies absenteeism doubled, rising to more than 10 percent on Mondays and Fridays. Walter Reuther, then president of the United Auto Workers, shortly before his death focused on the problem of the young worker. He said that these workers feel that they are not masters of their own destiny on the job and they are going to escape from it whenever they have an opportunity. Young workers then were interested in a sense of fulfillment as human beings. And they still are to a large extent today.

As the economy lagged, young people did tend toward a more conservative stance. But the landmark settlement between the auto workers and their industry in 1973 overcame the traditional focus of labor contracts on wages, monetary benefits, and mechanical working conditions. The contract between the UAW and Chrysler Corporation, for instance, in September 1973 gave emphasis to the workers' freedom of choice as to how they would spend their time after the regular eight-hour day. From Chrysler's point of view, the issue involved a cherished management prerogative—the right to require employees to work longer than their regular shifts if necessary to meet the demands of production.

During the negotiations the new UAW president, Leonard Woodcock, said, "We are challenging, in effect, whether human beings exist for the sake of production and profit, or whether we are engaged in production for the sake of human beings."

The *New York Times* said, "For the first time, a major industrial union achieved contractual guarantees aimed at improving the quality of a worker's life, rather than simply fattening his wallet."

Other factors in the automobile industry agreement gave union members a voice concerning questions of health and safety conditions in the plant. With regard to reducing boredom on the assembly line, the union won the right to participate in experimental projects. For example, workers were given autonomous responsibility for techniques used to manufacture engines. Some were allowed to organize the job themselves as they saw fit, supervising themselves, and for awhile worked at their own pace. They were held accountable only for delivering the finished product at the right time.

Rapidly evolving technology and the obsolescing of skills contribute to rapid change in the world of work. On both counts, the pace of change is increasing. Not only has technology restructured many jobs, but the change in society at large has also had an impact on the job. As then Secretary of Labor Willard Wirtz said in 1967, "Over the years the changing nature of work has been the cause of the greatest continuing restructuring of American lives of any major force in our history."

There is another side to work which must not be overlooked. For many persons, work is a vital part of the process of coping with life stress. This has two aspects: first, without work, the potential for boredom and meaninglessness is immeasurably increased. Work is often the primary means by which a person feels useful in life and through which significance and personal identity are established. The young adult must find a useful and meaningful place in society, and only in this way does a man or woman develop a firm sense of identity.

Second, work is often a form of coping and a refuge. Consider, for example, how people in grief regard work. Many report that in the process of mourning and reorienting their lives after a major loss, work is not a burden, but the best refuge against constant high levels of distress and depression. One speaks here of "burying one's self in work." Thus work may provide a psychological haven against problems that otherwise would be insurmountable, or against loneliness and depression. For such people *not* to work is to be deprived of the only viable means of coping with non-work-related stress.

We see this even more among women than among men. Women today are entering the work force in unprecedented numbers. This is perhaps the most significant sociological change in the world of work in this century. Work appears to be an increasingly attractive alternative to housewifery as a major occupation. Indeed, more than half the adult women in America have entered or returned to the work place. For many work is an economic necessity; for others it provides a useful supplement to the family income and enables the family to raise its standard of living. More important, it provides a psychological base away from home and both symbolic and real autonomy and independence. And as that independence is increasingly sanctioned by society, today's woman often needs the security of work to "be her own person."

Thus, although traditionally we tend to focus attention on work as a source of stressful *demands* or pressures, we need to realize that the work setting is often fruitful as a psychological resource.

SUMMARY

The stressors in the work setting are pervasive but are perceived differently by each person exposed to a given situation. Some react; some don't. One person's stressor seems to be another person's stimulus. Chapters 2 to 6, the core of the book, explain these individual differences. While the last three chapters may stand by themselves as material designed to give practical application to theory and observation and research, an understanding of my frame of reference in the next five chapters will provide the basis for the suggestions and the tools for self-evaluation.

Change and technical progress, both necessary to today's work, are the common denominator of stressors to which people react. The more work changes, the more it is seen as stressful. And while employers may have a legal liability to "pick up the pieces" and to pay for injury, there is an overriding moral and social responsibility to understand, to appreciate individual vulnerability, and to take measures to protect employees where possible and, often, to provide therapeutic resources where preventive measures are not possible.

I used a broad brush in this chapter to illustrate a wide variety of research which illustrates the relationship between occupational stress and stress reactions. Comments on the changing world of work will be expanded in Chapter 4 to extend the scene. Illustrative case examples further highlight the scope of our topic and begin to suggest both preventive and intervention strategies.*

REFERENCES

Gardell, Bertil (1975). Technology, alienation and mental health. Report Number 45, The Laboratory for Clinical Stress Research, Karolinska Institute, Stockholm, 1975.

Lesser, Philip J. (1967). The legal viewpoint. In A. McLean (ed.), *To Work Is Human.* New York: Macmillan.

Levi, Lennart (1974). Stress, distress and psychosocial stimuli. In A. McLean (ed.), *Occupational Stress.* Springfield: Charles C. Thomas.

---

* Other than those cases of public record, individuals described in this book represent composites with the experiences of each person described in amalgam of several whom I and my colleagues have seen over the years.

2

THE DYNAMICS
OF PSYCHOSOMATIC
REACTION

In this chapter I will examine some of the fascinating mechanisms that come into play between the disruptive stressor and the stress reaction. How do our bodily processes translate external events into physical symptoms? What is the relationship between such illnesses as ulcers or high blood pressure or heart disease and external circumstances? For that matter, what is meant by the term "psychosomatic medicine"?

HISTORICAL DEVELOPMENTS

The scientific foundation for the practice of medicine is a fairly recent development. The cornerstones were laid by Rudolph Virchow, a German physician who demonstrated typical microscopic tissue changes for a number of different diseases, and Louis Pasteur, his French contemporary whose work led to the realization that bacteria can cause disease. Their seminal efforts took place in the late nineteenth century and led to the scientific theory of the origin of disease.

Their discoveries concentrated professional interest on the *physical processes* in the human body. Doctors literally put the patient's body under the microscope and examined it in detail and, for the most part, ignored or segregated as a separate area of concern the patient's mental and emotional state and psychological and social background. Patterns of thought, feeling, and behavior, which could not be studied with the help of the microscope or by any other *biological* method, were largely ignored in the treatment of disease.

The great French physiologist Claude Bernard, in the second half of the nineteenth century—well before anyone thought of stress—first explained that the internal environment—or *milieu interiore*—of a living organism must remain fairly constant, despite changes in its external environment. He believed that this fixity of the *milieu interiore* is the condition of free and independent life. Some fifty years later, the distinguished American physiologist Walter B. Cannon suggested the term "homeostasis" (from the Greek *homoios*, meaning similar and *stasis*, meaning position), to describe this ability to stay the same or static.* What both men were saying, in other words, is that for an organism to maintain health it must maintain an internal balance. Every direction of the organism must be to maintain the healthy life of each aspect of the organism and each aspect of the organism must make great effort to remain within normal limits or return to normal at the earliest possible time when stretched beyond its normal shape or function.

Then Cannon went further. As early as 1909 he introduced the still useful theory that one reacts to stressors with physical preparation to fight or to flee.

> *There is no doubt that just as the secretory activity of the stomach is affected in similar fashion in man and in lower animals, so likewise gastric and intestinal peristalsis are stopped in man as they are stopped in lower animals, by worry and anxiety . . . indeed, the feeling of heaviness in the epigastrium commonly complained of by nervous persons may be due to the stagnation of food. That such stagnation occurs is shown in the following case.*

> *A refined and sensitive woman who had digestive difficulties, came with her husband to Boston to be examined. They went to a hotel for the night. The next morning the woman appeared at the consultant's office an hour after having eaten a test meal. An examination of the gastric contents revealed no free acid, no digestion of the test breakfast, and the presence of a considerable amount of the supper from the previous evening. The explanation of this stasis of food in the stomach came from the family doctor who reported that the husband had made the visit to the city an occasion for becoming uncontrollably drunk, and that he had by*

---

* Those familiar with systems theory or control theory would recognize this as "dynamic equilibrium."

his escapades given his wife a night of turbulent anxiety. The next morning, after the woman had had a good rest, the gastric contents were again examined; the proper acidity was found, and the test breakfast had been normally digested and discharged.

(CANNON, 1909).

Cannon's observations stimulated considerable research and speculation and an increasing number of physicians began to consider important the individual's social environment and living conditions and emotions. More and more, medical researchers and practitioners began to believe that successful treatment would have to take into account the whole person and his or her environment—not merely diseased organs.

During the first few decades of this century there was widespread application of the scientific methods of the mathematical and physical sciences to the biological sciences and to medicine in general. Nevertheless, a truly systematic study of the relationship between life events and the bodily reaction did not begin until the early 1940s. There was, to be sure, vast literature replete with observations and theory, but the kind of hard data which satisfies the scholars was absent. The real stimulus for the application of scientific methods—the spark that ignited the chain reaction of investigational energy—resulted from an encounter between two researchers and a seemingly unimpressive small man named Tom.

Tom, who was compelled to live with his stomach opened and connected to the surface of his body, was the subject of the studies and observations of Stewart Wolf and Harold Wolff at New York Hospital. The doctors carefully documented the color of Tom's stomach's lining, its motility, and its secretions as he underwent a great many stressful and reassuring life events. As Walter Cannon said in the foreword to Wolf and Wolff's 1943 report, "The functions of the stomach have never been investigated with the detailed care, the skill and the ingenuity, that have been displayed in the researches carried out by the authors."

The subject was a sensitive, proud, and independent individual, at times anxious, fearful, difficult, and obstinately decisive. His emotional range and responsiveness permitted discriminations which the authors fully documented. Through observing Tom, it became evident to Wolf and Wolff that frustration and repressed conflict were associated with increased blood flow in the stomach and with an increase in its motility and secretion. Likewise, it was evident that engorgement of the stomach lining, whatever its cause, was associated with less resistance to psychological trauma—and this was a major contribution to our understanding of the incidence of gastric ulcers.

The accident that led to Tom's condition (which, of course, made studies possible) occurred when Tom was nine years old. A neighboring saloon-keeper offered Tom's father some hot clam chowder. The father carried it home in an insulated beer pail, depositing it in the kitchen, and went out a few seconds later. Tom, who was thirsty from playing outdoors, came into the kitchen and, seeing the pail, grasped it by the top which was still cold. Thinking he was sneaking cold beer, he took a very large mouthful of the extemely hot liquid. He was afraid to spit it on the floor because he feared reprisals from his mother so he swallowed it. For an instant, he felt an intense burning sensation in his mouth, throat, and abdomen, and then he fell unconscious to the floor. His mother heard the crash and came down. He was brought to New York Hospital where attempts to keep his esophagus from becoming sealed off with scar tissue failed. The year was 1895.

Finally it became necessary to open the stomach to connect it to the abdominal wall in order for Tom to feed himslf. Thereafter he fed himself through the artificial opening.

As a result of his later work as a ditch digger, the tight-fitting gauze dressing covering the opening injured the edges of the exposed stomach. He was again treated at New York Hospital.

Two years after this experience, he was persuaded to become a subject for a research investigation. He was given a job as an assistant and handyman at New York Hospital laboratories, work he completed in the afternoons. In the mornings he came to the laboratory without having eaten and observations were made which led to a monumental advance in our understanding of bodily reactions to stressors.

The fact that emotional disturbances are associated with malfunctioning in the digestive system had been known for centuries. We have long known that armies "travel on their stomachs." The familiar empty feeling in the pit of the stomach and accompanying fear, lack of appetite, nausea, and vomiting often encountered at times of marked anxiety are also well known. A quantitative, scientific approach to these alterations had been attempted only once before, by one of Tom's researchers (Wolff) and a colleague.

The emotionally charged situations were not experimentally induced but were spontaneously occurring life problems and conflicts. Some of these involved situations arising from time to time in the laboratory. Others occurred in the setting of Tom's home life. Thirty-four separate situations were studied. Here are three examples.

1   A member of the staff suddenly entered the room. He began hastily opening drawers, looking on shelves, and swearing to himself as he searched for documents which were extremely valuable to him. Tom, who had cleaned up the laboratory the afternoon before, had mislaid them. He was fearful of detection and fearful of losing his job. He remained silent and motionless and his face became pallid. The mucous membrane of his stomach also blanched—on a redness scale from 0 to 10 it blanched from 9 to 2—and remained so for five minutes until the doctor had located the objects of his search and left the room. Then the gastric mucosa gradually resumed its former color.

2   The final observations relate to feelings of depression. Sadness, discouragement, and self-reproach were found to be associated with prolonged pallor of the stomach mucosa and a hypo secretion of acid. On one occasion it was noted that an actual inhibition in the customary digestive processes occurred during a period of mood depression. Once, when Tom was threatened by a depressing personal problem, the researchers found an inhibition of secretory activity and vascularity.

3   One day Tom spent in the outpatient clinics of the hospital. The next morning he came to the laboratory red faced with anger and brimming over with feelings of resentment and hostility against a certain clinic secretary and strong feelings of humiliation as well. He had had to do a good deal of running back and forth carrying various slips of paper here and there. Having come to regard himself as somewhat privileged at the hospital and therefore immune from routine abuse, he had had the impulse to quit the whole thing and return to the laboratory. But he stuck it out. At the completion of the clinic studies he was detained by a secretary in the last clinic. Although he remonstrated, she refused to let him go. Apparently she became irritable and then vindictive. Tom, humiliated and strongly resentful, stood waiting in silence.

The following morning when he came to the laboratory bursting with resentment his stomach was found to be in the condition one might expect to find in a person about to devour a big meal. "I wish I could get my hands on her neck," he said. The lining of his stomach was engorged and much redder than usual. The level of gastric secretions in terms of volume and acidity was three times normal.

For the first half hour Drs. Wolf and Wolff discussed the experi-

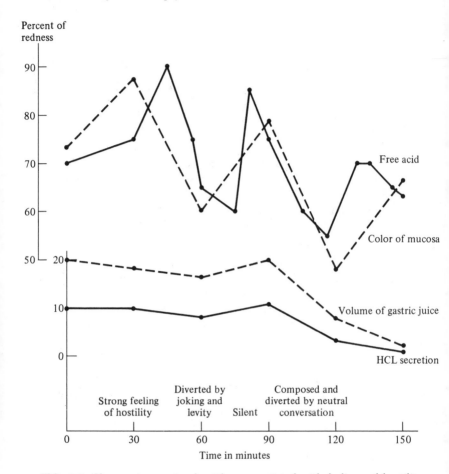

FIG. 2.1 *Changes in gastric physiology associated with feelings of hostility (Wolf and Wolff, 1943).*

ence with Tom in a rather unsympathetic fashion and were able to increase his hostility and at the same time accentuate the effects observed in his stomach. They then diverted him and were successful in relieving his hostile feelings. The engorgement and redness of the mucous membrane subsided perceptibly. See Fig. 2.1.

I think most of my colleagues would agree that the study of Tom inaugurated the scientific study of psychosomatic medicine. The scientific method moved previously speculative psychosomatic medicine toward acceptance by most physicians and toward the mainstream of medical practice.

Many other experiments in psychosomatic medicine were conducted by Dr. Wolff and his colleagues at New York Hospital. One example will illustrate in a compelling way much that is important in understanding occupational stress.

When embarrassed, many of us will blush. When angry, many also tend to become flushed. This commonplace psychosomatic relationship led to the study of capillary blood vessels (the smallest ones dilate to produce a flush). Techniques were developed rather easily to measure the so-called capillary tone (how contracted or expanded such vessels may be at any time).

In one experiment, capillary tone was measured in both arms. The research subject was then struck a painful blow on the left arm. The capillary tone in the arm dropped rapidly, as it did in the right arm, even though it had not been struck. Before long the tone returned to normal and after it did the experiment was repeated, except that this time the blow was halted less than an inch away from the arm. Although in this case the arm was not touched at all, the capillaries themselves again displayed a decreased tone—perhaps a defensive reaction. When during the third experiment, the individual was told that the blow would not be "real," there was *no* capillary reaction in *either* arm. This simple experiment helps us to understand the "near miss" reaction when we are faced with a potentially threatening physical accident that does not actually take place but which we *believe* might. When we anticipate physical trauma that does not materialize, we still react—often with physical symptoms.

Gradually it became clear that nature does not know any strict distinction between "functional" and "organic" interrelationships between mind and body. They are clearly intertwined. Alcohol and other drugs, brain tumors, and strokes all assault the brain in a very physical way but produce mental, emotional, and behavioral changes. This had been well known and accepted for many years before the work of Wolf and Wolff. Physicians began to suspect that functional disorders of probable emotional origin and of long duration may gradually lead to serious organic disorders associated with physical changes. A few instances of this kind have been known for a very long time—for example, the facts that hyperactivity of the heart may lead to enlarged heart muscles and that hysterical paralysis of a limb may lead to certain degenerative changes of muscles and joints because of inactivity. Physicians had to reckon with the possibility that a functional disorder of long duration in any organ could lead to definite anatomical changes and to symptoms of disability within that structure. As Franz Alexander, perhaps the leading psychoanalytic scholar of mind-body relationships of his time, put it in 1950:

> *Fear, aggression, guilt, frustrated wishes, if repressed, result in permanent and chronic emotional tensions which disturb the functions of the vegetative organs. Because of the complications of our social life, many emotions cannot be expressed and relieved freely through involuntary activities but remain repressed and are eventually diverted into an appropriate channel. Instead of being expressed in voluntary innervations, they influence the vegetative functions, such as digestion, respiration and circulation. Just as countries thwarted in their external political ambitions often experience internal social upheavals, so the human organism too may show a disturbance of its internal politics, of its vegetative functions, if its relation to the world is disturbed.*
>
> *This psychosomatic approach to the problem of life and disease brings internal physiological processes in the synthesis with the individual's relations to his social environment. It gives a scientific basis to empirical observations such as, for example, that a patient often shows marvelous recovery if he is removed from his family environment or if he interrupts his everyday occupations and thus is relieved of those emotional conflicts which stem from familial or professional relations. Detailed knowledge of the relationship between emotional life and bodily processes extends the function of the physician: physical and mental care of the patient can be coordinated into an integral whole of medical therapy. This is the real meaning of psychosomatic medicine. (pp. 47–48)*

WORLD WAR II

Other observations and research taking place at about the same time as Franz Alexander's comments and the publication of the studies of Tom give us a different perspective. From the laboratory and from theoretical observations, I want to illustrate much more direct reactions to the most seriously stressful situation people encounter in a direct way—war! The everyday reactions to life's customary conflicts are, as we have seen, often psychosomatic; the reactions to over-whelming threat also are often psychosomatic.

During the Second World War Roy Grinker and John Spiegel, two psychiatrists in the Army Air Force, made clinical observations of a large number of combat fliers in the European theater. Their careful observations of these men under stress included background details, personality characteristics, types of breakdown and a description of the day-to-day existence of hundreds of fliers. Their commentary from *Men Under Stress* (1945) will help to move our understanding of psychosomatic relationships and overt stress reactions toward another dimension.

> *The stress of war tries men as no other test that they may have encountered in civilized life. Like a crucial experiment it exposes the underlying physiological and psychological mechanisms of the human being. Cruel, destructive and wasteful though such an experiment may be, exceedingly valuable lessons can be learned from it regarding the methods by which men adapt themselves to all forms of stress, either in war or in peace. (p. vii)*

On psychological reaction to combat they say, "If the stress is severe enough, if it strikes an exposed 'Achilles heel' and if the exposure to it is sufficiently prolonged, adverse psychological symptoms may develop in anyone"(p. 53). They go on to point out that the symptoms which appear are based on individual personality characteristics of the flier and of the earlier experiences of the soldier in question.

> *The unending strain eventually produces distress signals affecting any part of the mind or body. Enthusiasm and eagerness easily give way to a great weariness of battle, which is then endured because there is no way out. Transient fears turn into permanent feelings of apprehension. Anxiety may be related for a time only to a reaction limited to the most dangerous moments over the target, but it has a tendency to spread until it is continuous or is stimulated by only trivial sounds. Good muscular coordination is replaced by uncontrolled tremors, jerky manipulations and tension. Constant tension leads further to restlessness which is never satisfied by activity and is intolerant of repose. Sleep dwindles and may give way altogether to insomnia punctuated by fitful nightmares. Appetite is noticeably reduced, and gastric difficul-*

ties may appear. Although air sickness is rare, nausea and vomit-ing after meals, especially breakfast, are fairly common, as is functional diarrhea. . . . With the growing lack of control over the mental and physical reactions come a grouchiness and irri-tability that interfere with good relations among men. Some give way easily, and are always in a quarrel or argument. Others become depressed and seclusive, and stay away from their friends to avoid dissension, or because they feel ashamed. Thinking and behavior may become seriously altered. Forgetfulness, preoccu-pation, or constant brooding over loss of friends in combat experiences destroy purposeful activity. The behavior of the men may become not only a social, but completely inappropriate and bizarre. (p. 54)

In many ways Grinker and Spiegel laid the groundwork for clin-ical methods of studying occupational stressors and psychosomatic reactions to them. We constantly collect case examples of workers reacting to psychosocial stressors in their environment with emotional disability. And the range of reaction, though not so universally extreme, is the same in principle as that seen among fliers during World War II. In all these cases, reactions are based upon the under-lying personality characteristics of the individual; they vary according to the duration of exposure to the stressor, the severity, and the par-ticular vulnerability of each person. They often start as or are most clearly manifest by psychosomatic disorder.

Wartime experiences sometimes have a lasting effect carrying over into one's civilian employment. An applicant for a sales position completed graduate work at an Ivy League business school following his return from Viet Nam. He then sought a position as a marketing representative in one of the largest food-distributing companies. Dur-ing his preplacement medical examination he was asked to take a rou-tine hearing test. Although no hearing defect was evident in casual conversation, the audiometer noted a marked deficit in both ears and in all audio frquencies. The technician reviewing the results with him became alarmed when he broke down and wept after hearing the results. She tried to reassure him. The physician who performed the subsequent medical examination was unable to draw him out about his reaction. He let the matter drop and rescheduled a follow-up examination three months hence. The new marketing representative repeatedly postponed his examination. Finally when the examination was rescheduled for the sixth time, he did appear for the appointment. He was obviously uncomfortable but went through with the procedure which again showed some hearing loss though not as great as at the time of the preplacement examination. Again he became tearful.

At the beginning of the interview with the occupational physician, he was outwardly open and expansive about his new position and prospective career. Soon he became silent, got up, and began pacing the office with clenched fists. For awhile he stared out the window and eventually tears again came to his eyes. After a full fifteen minutes, in a hesitating voice, he recalled that his father had "been unmerciful" with his mother when she became deaf, refusing to accept her disability. He then spoke of events during the Viet Nam war when "I heard things no one should ever hear."

With essentially no prompting from the doctor, he elaborated upon some extraordinarily gruesome events in Viet Nam which led to the deaths of women and children whom he saw and heard in the final moments of their lives. Although he has been trying to suppress these memories, he still wakes up at least once a week with a nightmare relating to the episodes and he still has some difficulty with his hearing acuity.

Here is a case of an individual who was sensitized early in life to the consequences of hearing deficit and who subsequently was faced with sounds which had to be put out of mind to maintain sanity. When the memories of those events occasionally surfaced he became acutely anxious; when partially surfaced he had bad dreams. The experience produced a hearing loss on a purely psychological basis— an example of psychosomatic reaction with understandable roots and readily measurable disability. With appropriate psychotherapy one would expect his hearing to return to normal.

FIGHT OR FLIGHT

Before proceeding, it would be useful to highlight an important footnote in psychosomatics and entertain a contemporary caution on the acceptance of a unitary cause of a psychosomatic or other stress reaction. Cannon's concept of the "fight or flight" reaction which he first described more than fifty years ago still has considerable currency. He pointed out that if our prehistoric ancestors unexpectedly were attacked by an aggressive wild animal their bodies would respond with a physical and psychological state which best prepared them to deal with the situation. Either they were prepared to attack or to run. Among other things, the heart would pound harder and faster, breathing would become deeper and more rapid, pupils would dilate, and they would become mentally more alert. Reaction would be almost instantaneous.

While we rarely encounter wild animals bent on our destruction these days, this generalized response to real and imagined stressors remains. And while our culture does not often allow us to physically attack the person, object, or event which mobilizes the preparatory response, that response remains and we often sense it as fear or anxiety. The same symptoms may be as easily aroused by the driver behind us leaning on the horn as by the perception of disapproval by one's teacher or one's boss. Each tends to mobilize the generalized stress response which in turn is expressed in uniquely individual ways. While the basic pattern is always the same, there are significant differences both in the degree of response and in the effects among individuals and in any one individual from time to time. Repeated exposure to a specific stressor may result in a conditioning of the individual to react in a stereotyped way. Such conditioning may be positive or negative, increasing or decreasing vulnerability to the specific stressor; it may raise or lower a reaction's threshold, enhancing or reducing one's tolerance to stress in general and improving or interfering with the rate of recovery from the stress reaction.

We do not have the final answer as to whether or not a stressful social condition or threatening interpersonal relationship can ever be the sole cause of symptoms or of a disease. As Dr. Lawrence Hinkle, Jr. (1974), Head of the Division of Human Ecology at Cornell, puts it:

> At a time when it is considered that the presence of microorganisms is not a sole and sufficient explanation for the occurrence of infectious disease, that the presence of abnormal genes is not a sole and sufficient explanation for the occurrence of genetic disease, that the experience of trauma is not a sole and sufficient explanation for the occurrence of traumatic disease, and that the availability of alcohol and narcotics is not a sole and sufficient explanation for the occurrence of alcoholism or drug addiction, it is unreasonable to suppose that exposure to a certain kind of interpersonal relationship or social condition will be found to be a sole and sufficient explanation for the occurrence of disease of any sort. The likelihood is that social phenomenon will inter-

*relate with other apparent 'causes.' One will indeed see hard-
working, striving, impatient men who drop dead suddenly at the
end of a hard day's work. If one performs population studies on a
prospective basis, one is likely to find that this occurs most frequently among middle-aged and elderly men who are hyperlipi-
demic,* who have elevated blood pressures, who have a long history of smoking cigarettes, and who have evidence of disorders of
their cardiac condition systems; and it will be very rare indeed
that such a sudden death will be found in a healthy young woman
who has none of these conditions. (pp. 355–356)*

TODAY'S RESEARCH

Research on life's stressors and their psychological and physiological
effects has by now become extraordinarily sophisticated. Specific
research reports range from broad epidemiological studies of patterns
of overt illness in large populations to investigations of specific biochemical and neuroendocrine changes in individual subjects. New
studies of the complex interplay between psychosocial stressors and
subtle changes in biochemical, endocrine and electrical systems in the
body suggest we are on the frontier once again of new understanding.
New tools of statistical analysis allow the collection of data simulta-
neously from a variety of stressors, from the social environment, and
from the research subjects and permit the structuring of experiments
to hold one or more set of variables nearly constant across all subjects
to control for a single set of measurements. These applications of what
are called "multivariate statistical methods" are now used along with
the older statistical methods of multiple regression, factor analysis,
cluster analysis, and discriminant analysis (Rubin 1974).

Also available today are new techniques of chemistry which
allow extremely complex analyses of hormone patterns. This permits
simultaneous measurement of different aspects of stress reactions. We
also have far more sophisticated psychosocial measurements of the
environment in which the stressor–stress reaction takes place. We find
ourselves with the tools which now and in the future will bring us
more understanding of the extraordinarily complicated relationship
between perceived occupational stressors and one's reaction to them.

---

* Excessive fatty acids in the blood.

In recent years psychosomatic research laboratories have flourished and theoretical considerations have become much more sophisticated. Let me cite some examples of contemporary stress research.

Techniques of coping with stress have also become more sophisticated and an exciting body of research and theoretical material has blossomed around them. Dr. Neal Miller, Professor of Psychology at Rockefeller University, comments that having a way to cope may reduce the physical effects of stress. He describes an experiment in which two groups of rats were subjected to the stress of repeated electric shocks; the first group was taught a way to control the number of shocks, but the second was not.

Although both groups received exactly the same shocks, the second group developed five times as many stomach lesions (similar to ulcers) as those who could control the situation. Dr. Miller suggests that there are implications for people from his studies with animals — that there are physical benefits in "turning worry into actions and plans."

Dr. Miller's experiments, and those of many others, suggest that the very process of taking action can reduce the unhealthy effects of stressful situations. If you are anxious about an upcoming meeting, for example, you will be better off if you prepare your materials and think things through ahead of time than if you sit and stew. "Actions and plans" will take the harmful edge off your physiological reactions whether they be in your stomach or elsewhere.

From another point of view, Dr. Richard Lazarus, Professor of Psychology at the University of California at Berkeley, also suggests that one's reaction to a stressful situation will vary with one's attitude. When elderly patients in one of his studies were moved to a nursing home he found that those who became depressed had a far poorer survival rate than those who became angry. And those who maintained a philosophical attitude about their new locale did very well indeed.

Hormone analysis of urine accumulated while a person is exposed to various stressful events gives us a useful and practical assessment of the degree of stress reaction within the organism at that time. If, at the same time, one also studies the productivity of different groups of people, together with their behavior, and their subjective feelings, it is possible to achieve a reasonably comprehensive assessment of the degree of stress present in these groups. In other words, it should be possible to estimate just how much a specific task demands and, conversely, just what resources the individual has to match the demands made upon him or her. Such a knowledge of the demands made by a job and of the individual's resources is obviously of vital importance to our understanding the ways to ensure the goodness of fit between a person and his or her work. This, in fact, was the chief concern of a series of experiments, conducted mainly by Dr. Lennart Levi who was then Director of the Stress Laboratories at the Karolinska Institute in Stockholm. Levi used one of the earliest quantitative scales of measurement of stress reaction comparing the amount of adrenaline and noradrenaline (the stress hormones producted by the sympathetic nervous system) present in the urine with the subject's own version of what he or she experienced during the period the urine was accumulated.

A research example of stress in working life proceeded as follows. Twelve women in the invoicing department of a large office were shown in the course of a work study to be capable of producing about 160 invoices per hour each. After they had been briefed on the nature of the procedures involved, their performance was surveyed during four consecutive working days. On the second and fourth days, the normal system of payments was followed—that is, a fixed monthly salary. On the first and third days, however, the system was suddenly switched to a high and rapidly progressive piece-work rate. The quicker and better they worked, the more steeply their incomes rose.

Productivity was assessed in terms of invoices per hour, with certain deductions for clerical errors. A check was maintained on physical conditions and on mental well-being by means of questionnaires filled out by the women every two hours. Three urine samples were collected from every woman regularly every day, and these were analyzed for adrenaline and noradrenaline content.

On the two piece-work days production rose on the average by 113 percent to 331 invoices per woman per hour. The incidence of mistakes, however, was no higher than previously.

There were side effects to the experiment, however. The feeling of strain increased significantly, the "fatigue index" nearly doubled. Nearly all the women complained of bodily sensations of discomfort such as pains in arms and shoulders and head and back which did not exist on salary-payment days. After the work on piece-work days the girls were physically and mentally exhausted.

The objective data—that is, the excretion of stress hormones— was significant. During the piece-work days the noradrenaline and adrenaline rose by 27 percent and 40 percent respectively. In short, Levi (1967) demonstrated that piece-work arrangements led to considerable rise in productivity but also gave rise to stress reactions which could be both subjectively *and* objectively measured. He concluded that

> *. . . one can reasonably suppose that, if this condition of stress had been allowed to continue, it would have broken out in the form of nervous complaints, increased muscular pains, low morale, a higher incidence of sick leave, and an increased turnover of personnel. The resultant losses would no doubt have been reserved for a separate ledger, far away from the immaculate statistics of increased hourly production. But the ultimate cost, in terms of company profits, national expenditure and human values, would not. (p. 83)*

This becomes important in the development of studies of occupational stress since it provides *objective* measurements of the way people react to stressful work situations. The more it becomes possible to *quantify* such reactions in a physiological sense, the less subjective complaints carry scientific validity. And yet Levi was fairly well able to demonstrate the relationship between the subjective complaints and the measurable physiological changes in reaction to stress.

REACTIONS TO FRUSTRATION

Given any stressful situation, such as continuing, discomforting job demands, everyone goes through a series of reactions in an effort to minimize the situation, to reduce the effects of stressors. At first we seek a logical and rational solution. Our feelings play a minor role. We look for the intelligent way out. Usually, in cases of less serious stressors, this works.

When no satisfactory solution develops from this approach, we cast about for other methods of resolving the situation. This leads to an increase in random activity. The most common example of this is the way we look for something recently lost. If an initial search does not locate it, our behavior tends to become erratic. We repeatedly circle the room, looking into the same closets and nooks again and again, becoming more disturbed each time around. This behavior is illogical. Our feelings of frustration, irritation, and annoyance call forth unreasonable patterns of random activity. It may nonetheless lead us to finding the lost object; to a stress-reducing solution.

Failing that, however, we may become unrealistically angry or begin to internalize the anger and frustration. This often aggressive behavior is not necessarily directed against the source of stress; sometimes it is maldirected at a substitute. Often if it cannot be expressed directly it comes out in psychosomatic symptoms such as headache, gastrointestinal symptoms, and generalized feelings of tension. At other times we blame others.

Take, for example, the case of an executive promoted well beyond his level of competence who clearly recognized at the time of his most recent promotion that he was over his head. He sought competent assistants who would be able to provide the expertise to "bail him out" both from the technical and the managerial aspects of the functions for which he was now responsible. He brought in consultants. He became increasingly frustrated and angry with himself and his associates as he saw his unit of the business begin to founder. Then he experienced a reactivation of disabling headaches, which he had not experienced for fifteen years. They eventually became so severe and chronic that he was unable to maintain the attendance, let alone performance, necessary to remain in his new assignment. Within a week of his transfer to a staff position the headaches, anger, and frustration disappeared. In this instance the staff job proved an ideal fit and a psychosomatic cure. While the solution to psychosomatic reactions is rarely so simple an environmental manipulation, such relief is not uncommon when removal from a stressful situation is possible.

HANS SELYE

I am concluding this chapter on psychosomatics with comment on the work of a leading stress researcher which illustrates the close interrelationship between psychosomatic relationships and individual reactions to stressors. Even this brief description demonstrates the relationship between specific stressors and psychosomatic reactions to them in the stress equation. It is also readily apparent that Selye's work builds upon Cannon's concepts of "fight or flight."

Probably no single individual has contributed more to both scientific and popular thinking on stress than Hans Selye, Professor and Director of the Institute of Experimental Medicine and Surgery at the University of Montreal. With 28 books and 1,400 articles to his credit, he is far and away the field's most prolific author. His more recent writings range from a brief popular paperback (Selye, 1974) to a 1,256-page encyclopedic summary of the field for the serious student (Selye, 1976).

An understanding of Selye's original and more recent concepts of stress is necessary to round out this brief summary of psychosomatic relationships. It is also important to advise the reader who wants to further explore stress concepts of an important body of work which has strongly influenced many contemporary stress scholars. Indeed, some would say that Selye introduced the modern use of the word "stress." But he did so with a definition that is somewhat narrower than that found in the preface to this book and its successors. While you will recall that the authors in this series use the word to define the process or the system which includes the stressful event and the reaction to it and all the intervening steps as well, Selye's use of the term gives heavy emphasis to the stress reaction.

Stress in Selye's terms is the nonspecific *response* of the body to *any* demand made upon it. In explaining this concept he points out that each demand made upon our bodies is in a sense unique; that is, it is *specific*. When exposed to cold, we shiver to produce more heat and our skin blood vessels contract to reduce the loss of heat from body surfaces. And with heat, we sweat because evaporation of perspiration has a cooling effect. A major muscular effort such as running makes increased demands upon musculature and the cardiovascular system. The muscles need supplementary energy to perform their usual work; hence the heart beats more rapidly and strongly and blood pressure rises to dilate the vessels, therefore increasing the flow of blood to the muscles.

And each drug or hormone has specific actions. Adrenaline augments pulse rate; insulin decreases blood sugar. Yet no matter what kind of derangement is produced, all these agents have one thing in common; they also increase the demand for readjustment. This demand is nonspecific; it requires adaptation to a particular problem, regardless of what that problem may be. In other words, in addition to their specific effects, all agents and events to which we are exposed also produce a *nonspecific* increase in the need to perform *adaptive* functions and therefore to re-establish normalcy. As Selye (1974) says:

> From the point of view of its stress-producing or stressor activity,
> it is immaterial whether the agent or situation we face is pleasant

or unpleasant; all that counts is the intensity of the demand for readjustment or adaptation. The mother who is suddenly told that her only son died in battle suffers a terrible mental shock; if years later it turns out that the news was false and the son unexpectedly walks into the room alive and well, she experiences extreme joy. The specific results of the two events, sorrow and joy, are completely different, in fact, opposite to each other, yet their stressor effect—the nonspecific demand to readjust herself to an entirely new situation—may be the same. (p. 15)

What Selye has clearly done is demonstrate that such essentially different things as cold, heat, drugs, hormones, sorrow, and joy can provoke an identical biochemical reaction in the body. By means of highly objective quantitative biochemical determinations he showed that certain reactions are totally nonspecific and common to all types of exposure. In the 1930s he named this the "general adaptation syndrome." He pointed out that it is not necessary that the G.A.S. produces harmful effects. Instead, its effect depends merely on the intensity of the demand made on the adaptive capacity of the body. As he says, "Any kind of normal activity—a game of chess or even a passionate embrace—can produce considerable stress without causing any harmful effects" (p. 18).*

SUMMARY

In these first two chapters the broad range of severity of stressful events and conditions to which we are heir has become very apparent. Many are trivial; some overpowering. Equally apparent, stress reactions range from a barely perceptible increase in pulse rate to disabling physical and emotional illness.

While it is important to keep in mind the inextricably close and involved relationship between mind and body, between feelings and the world around us, and while we need to be aware of the very serious and disabling reactions that sometimes occur, the focus of this book is on job stress. Since the overwhelming majority of stressful events at work do not produce disease, the emphasis in the next few chapters will be on these more common reactions to stressful aspects of work.

---

* Lennart Levi's volume in this series, *Preventing Work Stress,* will elaborate on Dr. Selye's theoretical concepts.

REFERENCES

Alexander, F. (1950). *Psychosomatic Medicine.* New York: Norton.

Cannon, W. B. (1909). The influence of emotional states on the functions of the Alimentary canal. *The American Journal of Science* **137**: 480–487.

Grinker, Roy R. and John P. Spiegel (1945). *Men Under Stress.* Philadelphia: Blakiston.

Hinkle, L. E., Jr. (1974). The concept of "stress" in the biological and social Sciences. *International Journal of Psychiatry in Medicine:* **5** (4): 335–357, p. 355–56. Copyright held by the Baywood Publishing Company, 43 Central Drive, Farmingdale, New York 11735.

Levi, L. (1967). *Stress: Sources, Management and Prevention.* New York: Liveright.

Rubin, Robert T. (1974). Biochemical and neuroendocrine responses to severe psychological Stress. In E. K. E. Gunderson and R. H. Rahe, *Life, Stress and Illness.* Springfield: Charles C. Thomas.

Selye, H. (1974). *Stress Without Distress.* New York: J. B. Lippincott.

Selye, H. (1976). *Stress in Health and Disease.* Boston: Butterworths.

Wolf, Stewart, and Harold G. Wolff (1943). *Gastric Function: An Experimental Study of a Man and His Stomach.* New York: Oxford University Press.

3
CONTEXT, VULNERABILITY, AND SPECIFIC STRESSORS

In the past it has not been easy for executives, even those who are aware of their own personal reactions to stressful events in their own jobs, to accept the idea that work can adversely affect both mental and physical health. But there now is mounting interest in what has come to be called "job stress" and even "executive stress." Many leaders are asking intelligent questions about how their organizations affect employee health.

In what contexts are specific stressors most apt to produce symptoms? What seems to sensitize individuals to make them more susceptible to stressors? How can we identify these factors or, for that matter, the incidence of the symptom clusters we call illness in the work population at risk?

How can we organize our thinking about the complex interaction that exists between the individual's ever-changing vulnerability and the varying pressures on the job? This chapter will introduce one way to do so which will serve as the frame of reference for the rest of the book.

As I see it, two factors help to determine if a specific stressor will produce symptoms. The first is the *context* (or external environment) in which the interaction takes place. Even more important is the particular *vulnerability* of the individual at the time.

The social, physical, or psychological environment (or context) may be as broad as an economy or as small as a family unit. It may be industry wide or limited to a single organization or to one department of a plant within an organization. In a work setting, the context is also set by management policy and practice.

During an economic recession when there is loss of employment, for example, stressors may be much more significant to the individual than they would be when economic security is not threatened. The closing of a factory or an industry leads to vast disruption and changes in life-style. And activity of the family unit can be a supportive or a destructive environmental system.

INDIVIDUAL VULNERABILITY

Individual vulnerability to specific stressors varies widely and it is even more important than context in determining reaction to factors in a work environment. The enduring personality characteristics of a person are elements in setting the dimensions of vulnerability and we must therefore recognize both genetic and developmental influences that stamp each of us as unique. At the same time, we clearly recognize that these characteristics will vary as other factors change.

For instance, one's vulnerability alters with age. As Roy Grinker, Sr., points out, individual "coping . . . may be related to the failures of an individual's life cycle, particularly . . . phases involving and including the social aspects of change. In general, it appears that each such phase has its own pattern or organization, its own vulnerabilities, and its own methods of coping" (Grinker, 1974, p. xii).

Vulnerability also changes according to day-to-day events, moods, and individual experiences. One's role in a particular setting, one's perception of the expectations held of him or her by others, and one's perceived ability to control or alter the situation are important factors in understanding how specific stressors are interpreted and what reactions or coping mechanisms are evoked.

Stressors in this scheme are defined in terms of producing symptoms only when the context and vulnerability are ripe. That is, one must be particularly vulnerable or be in a generally threatening environment to have a specific stressor produce symptoms, unless, of course, the stressor is enormously powerful. It is therefore difficult to categorize such factors. They are quite literally defined in terms of vulnerability and context.

Stimulus conditions that evoke responses have been described by many. Some of these stressors produce sufficiently pathological adaptation to be considered the precipitators of symptoms of disease.

However, the nature of the environment or context and of the vulnerability of the organism are what give potency to the stressor.

Every event that I have examined as a specific stressor appears to involve *change* in some way. Changes frequently occur in supervisors, tasks, or comfortable routines. Or the stressor may be a factor in the work environment which has not itself changed but which becomes productive of a symptom when vulnerability is sharply increased.

One way to illustrate the relationship between context, vulnerability, stressors, and symptoms is through the use of moving, at times overlapping circles (see Fig. 3.1). The three circles here represent the three components I have been discussing. The area where all three overlap may be thought of as the individual's *symptomatic* response.

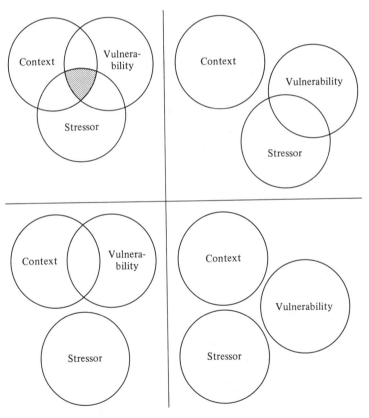

FIG. 3.1 *Symptomatic relationships between context, vulnerability, and stressors.*

As one views the illustration, each circle should be thought of as moving *away from and/or toward* the others depending on the importance of each of the three groups of variables. They are in constant and fluid motion. Each varies symbolically in size and with time. If the symbolic circle of vulnerability has shifted away from the others (to the right) so there is no overlap, there would be no symptoms. The same obtains for environmental factors if the context circle moves to the left. In this scheme contextual or environmental factors obviously play a contributory role in the development of symptoms. One can withstand otherwise destructive stressors if the context is supportive and the vulnerability is low. This will serve as a very simplistic model or framework for the rest of this volume.

ORGANIZATIONAL STRESSORS, JOB SATISFACTION, AND ANXIETY

Several years ago, a large manufacturing company decided upon a new product line which would involve the development, manufacture, marketing, installation, and service of extremely sophisticated machinery. New manufacturing techniques and processes had to be created. The marketing unit was faced with the need to deal with a product line more complicated than any predecessor. Technicians and service personnel had to master the art of installation and service of the machinery.

As with the introduction of any new process or product, adaptation to the challenges and problems associated with its introduction are first felt in the development laboratories, then in the manufacturing facilities, then in the market place, and then in customer locations. The need to adapt moves in waves across an organization and many a work unit is affected by the force which results. So also are the many individuals within those units, in this case most particularly those in management. The decision was therefore made to try to understand more clearly some of the stressors acting upon the management system and the individuals who were a part of it. The idea was to identify the specific pressures faced by these individuals with a view toward moderating them if at all possible.

A questionnaire was prepared and pretested. It examined satisfaction with work, perceived stress of specific tasks, and the extent of specific physical and emotional problems. Some twenty questions also centered on anxiety levels. All questions were structured to compare the participants' current feelings with their feelings on the same issues three years before. Questionnaires were returned anonymously.

In the first sample, questionnaire data were analyzed from 865 managers, for 898 managers 18 months later, and for 1,500 managers 18 months thereafter. Table 3.1 represents the population sample for the last study. Since I will focus specifically on the *manufacturing, marketing,* and *service divisions,* it might be helpful to keep these groups of managers in mind. We will be considering responses from 247 marketing managers, 193 service managers, and 195 managers in factory locations. Several of the other divisions in the work organization were not affected by the new product; others were, but to a lesser degree. They are not included in this discussion.

TABLE 3.1 *Management stress study population sample*

Division	No. of managers	Approx. % in study	No. of question- naires mailed	No. of question- naires returned	% of question- naires returned
Marketing	2390	15%	360	247	69%
Service	1544	15%	230	193	84%
Manu- facturing	1740	15%	260	195	75%
Totals			850	635	76%

It was interesting to trace the responses of management in the different groups over time. (These responses are graphically illustrated in the next four figures.) The first two questions have to do with perception of stressfulness of the company (see Fig. 3.2). In each case the manager was asked to give a rating on a five-point scale from "much more stressful" to "much less stressful." The top two classifications of "much more stressful" and "somewhat more stressful" were combined to give the percentages shown.

In this and subsequent figures the original population was, unfortunately, not sufficiently differentiated to give separate figures for the three groups. Note that those responsible for manufacturing felt the company was much less stressful after 36 months than at 18 months. At 18 months, 81 percent felt the company was much more or somewhat more stressful than three years prior, and at 36 months, only 60 percent did. The marketing group's perception of stressfulness rose

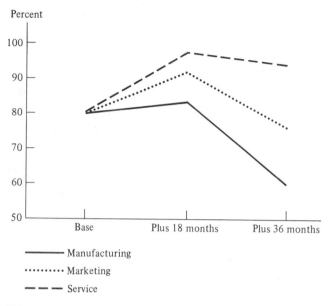

FIG. 3.2 *"Rate company compared with three years ago"—much more and somewhat more stressful.*

considerably at 18 months to 89 percent and dropped at 36 months to a still relatively high level of 77 percent. The service managers' perception of stressfulness also rose dramatically as they became enmeshed in learning about and installing the first pieces of equipment and it remained very high at 36 months. *Remember, this group is customarily last to feel the impact of new processes.*

There was less disparity in responses to questions about the stressfulness of "your job." The trend lines, however, were essentially similar. Those managers in factories showed a gradual reduction in perception of stressfulness. Those in marketing and in the service divisions rose and then eased off (see Fig. 3.3). Job satisfaction, although consistently very high during the entire period, followed the same trends as perception of job stressfulness.

Two of the questions which were used to get some feeling for anxiety level will conclude this brief illustration of applied management stress research. They seem to suggest one reason we found a high correlation between anxiety level, perception of increased stressfulness of work, and job dissatisfaction (see Fig. 3.4).

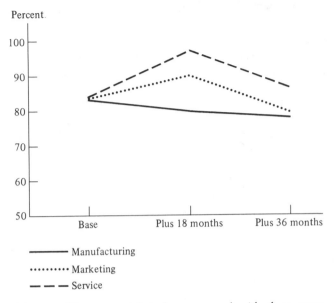

FIG. 3.3 *"Rate your job today compared with three years ago"—much more and somewhat more stressful.*

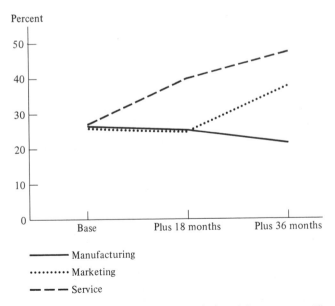

FIG. 3.4 *"Bothered by nervousness, feeling fidgety or tense?" —many times and pretty often.*

Of all the questions used, this question: "Are you bothered by nervousness, feeling fidgity or tense?" seemed to have the best correlation with clinical anxiety. Service managers moved from 26 percent to 37 percent to 46 percent over the four-year period while the manufacturing staff dropped to 20 percent at the end of the study.

Figure 3.5 conforms to the trends we saw earlier. That is, the manufacturing staff is less tense on the job, the service people are much more uncomfortable, and the marketeers seem to be less anxious.

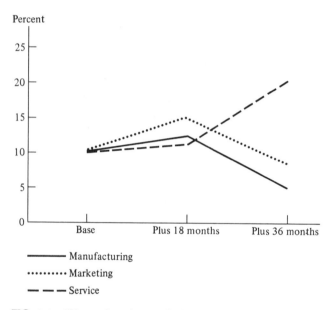

FIG. 3.5   "How often do you feel tense or nervous on the job?"
—always and usually.

We now generally accept a fairly high correlation between anxiety, perceptions of job stressfulness, and low morale. We strongly suspected that this was the case.

If you refer again to the model, the material here suggests a relationship between occupational stressors, context, and levels of anxiety. It does not address individual vulnerability. Let me turn to another study which unexpectedly turned out to do so.

OFF-THE-JOB STRESSORS

Meaningful data may frequently be obtained from cases seen in the work organization's medical departments. People who work in such units are accustomed to seeing individuals with psychiatric disorders who point to one or another aspect of their jobs as particularly discomforting. Often we see symptoms of psychiatric disability in an individual adapting to changes on the job. Changes at work that have been blamed include promotions, demotions, transfers, new management and new processes, technological change, and obsolescing skills. And they often *do* provoke unconscious sensitivitives leading to symptoms.

For some twenty years a colleague and I collected cases where severe emotional reactions apparently were precipitated by such changes in the work environment. Individuals were included in this sample when they met two criteria: (1) They suffered from incapacities caused by psychiatric illness which necessitated work absence, and (2) There occurred change at work immediately prior to the symptoms.

Some thirty-six patients met these qualifications and were included. Although this is *not* rigorous research but relatively "soft" clinical data, there were some remarkable similarities among the cases.

1   Although the patients worked for seven different firms and their occupations ranged from skilled craftsmen to corporate officials, certain common characteristics were apparent in the employee-employer relationship that could best be described as one of mutual dependency.

2   While the emotional reactions of the patients occurred in a setting of occupational change, they invariably developed at a time when the individual was adjusting to an unrelated personal stressor and was particularly vulnerable.

3   The length of time between these external circumstances and the time of the job change that triggered psychiatric illness was generally less than three months. External or contextual influences apparently strained the individual's ability to adapt, so the patient then turned for greater emotional support to his close relationship with the company. When that was disrupted by the change—a specific stressor—the patient was no longer able to cope successfully.

And so we see illustrated the relationship between stressors, vulnerability and symptoms (McLean, 1961).

PRACTICAL APPLICATIONS

How can one make practical application of this model of the ever-changing circles of occupational stress? Can one successfully construct a system to demonstrate practical interrelationships for the reader? How should one use this simple conceptual scheme as a teaching device for the embattled, stressed, abrasive manager or, for that matter the comfortable, the seemingly content and stable one? It seemed worthwhile to attempt self-assessment surveys and checklists to crudely measure individual vulnerability, one's personal context, and individual perceptions of specific stressors which may be active at any given point in time.

In Chapter 9, I will present more details of this self-assessment technique. There is considerable personal value in having a benchmark to measure, no matter how crudely, one's current stress status. Meanwhile, the next three chapters will explore in greater detail context, vulnerability, and specific stressors.

REFERENCES

Grinker, R. R., Sr. (1974). Foreword in G. V. Coelho, D. A. Hamburg, and J. E. Adams (eds.), *Coping and Adaptation.* New York: Basic Books.

McLean, A. A. (1961). Medical problems in employment continuity of senior citizens: from the viewpoint of the psychiatrist. *New York Journal of Medicine* 61 (17): 2901–2905.

McLean, A. A. (1976). *Dealing with Job-related Stress* (Cassette). Darien, Conn.: Management Decision Systems, Inc.

4

THE BROAD
SOCIAL CONTEXT

The broad psychosocial environment which makes up the arena that I refer to as context includes many aspects of the work environment. The physical setting, the health and safety practices of the employer, management attitudes toward employees, morale, the employee participation in decision-making processes—these factors and many more are vital elements of the context in which we work.

In this chapter I will quite deliberately go farther afield to explore the broader societal context which secondarily impacts the job arena. It is the influence of the community, the family, the economy, and society at large which the employee brings to work. These "secondary" influences are often lost sight of in comments on job stress. Nonetheless, attention must be paid to them. Workers do not leave the influences of their nonwork life at the plant or office door. And as these external influences change, so does the employee's attitude and behavior at work.

The broad social context in which an individual reacts in a healthy or unhealthy way is in part determined by such conditions as the state of the national and local economies. Economists almost universally predict serious instability with the likelihood of continuing inflation, more deficit financing, and unemployment reaching well into the 1980s. The reasons for this instability are many, and the factors responsible for it are no longer considered amenable to ready solution by political and fiscal manipulation of various financial and employment measures. The pressures of interest groups—politicians, unions, the business community, and, increasingly, the public at large—continue to hamper the management of stable economic policy. Economists too are unable to agree on a clear long-term picture.

This sense of unease has produced a pervasive insecurity which strongly colors the broad context of life to the point that vague external forces today loom far larger than they have during recent decades. Some claim that we are in the grip of a social crisis and are threatened with the collapse of democratic societies as a consequence of potential economic depression, unemployment, and instability. Others maintain that while such factors are necessary, they are not sufficient in and of themselves to cause such a collapse: there must also occur some loss of conviction in the animating ethos of a culture, some coming apart of the moral binder which holds men in the discipline of custom.

As I look at the many features of our environment that tend to establish a climate in which stressful events have great potency, I am struck by the overwhelming reality of job loss and the threat of job loss and the relationship in turn between job loss and ill health. The symbol of a job to identify with, of an employer/union/work group to call one's own, is high in our scale of values. When such relationships are threatened or disrupted the disordered life which follows for the worker and his or her family often contributes to real distress.

Brenner (1973) has clearly shown relationship between high unemployment rates and first admissions to mental hospitals. For the first time, in a definitive and scholarly study, he leaves little doubt about the correlation between mental disorder and the lack of work.

My focus in this chapter will be on the threat of unemployment as a major part of the context of far too many people and a factor with which we all must contend. Before dealing with the specifics of unemployment, however, a few contemporary issues that relate to work's context deserve consideration.*

---

* Job loss, of course, is a specific stressor. And unemployment contributes to one's vulnerability as well. What I will discuss here is the condition of being unemployed as part of one's psychosocial milieu. It may seem an artificial splitting, but it can dramatically illustrate the importance of external factors in the job-stress equation. There is a blurring between such stressful conditions as those encountered in Chapter 6 (specific occupations and factors intrinsic to a job) and the way in which I here treat the condition of unemployment as a contextual issue. Let me simply acknowledge that no model is perfect and get on with it.

CHANGING ATTITUDES TOWARD WORK

Employment itself is, of course, only one of several aspects of life that affect the lives of people in a broader society. Therefore, the work place should be viewed in the perspective of external change in the psychosocial environment, which has a specific bearing upon employee behavior and attitude on the job. A number of rapid changes are occurring in industrialized society which have direct consequences on the work scene. I would briefly cite the following nine issues as related to the work organizations and the adaptation of those enmeshed in them.

1 *Contemporary economic problems.* Workers in Western societies are persistently buffeted by a number of economic and social problems which affect their attitudes, their confidence, and their performance on the job. These include the relatively slow economic growth in recent years. While the 1960s were marked by expansive industrial growth in all of the Western countries, the worldwide recession of 1974–75 interrupted, and in some cases actually reversed, the rising productivity per employee. As unemployment rates began to improve, the energy crisis began. For the first time in four decades, government leaders in the West were using such terms as "depression" to describe the serious impact on production and on the labor force. The economic difficulties included underutilization of capital resources with substantial spare capacity, a reduction in productivity, balance of payment imbalances, reduced exports, painful inflationary pressures, and an enlarged burden of social costs to support the non-working population. Clearly, this atmosphere created an intensified fear of unemployment and fear of change among workers. In fact, today many countries are experiencing their worst combination of high unemployment, high inflation, and reduced productivity since the 1950s.

2 *The era of rising entitlements.* Western industrialized societies have been riding the crest of economic growth. Although this crest peaked in 1974, the deep-seated and almost universal expectations of rising standards of living have not diminished.

Europeans and Americans alike have cultivated the desire for a better life—and for more and more. Consumer appetites have been sharpened by the production and distribution of massive quantities of attractive goods, ranging from quick-frozen convenience foods to labor-saving machines in homes; the private automobile, including the two-car and three-car family; year-round and summer homes; and increased leisure and glamorous vacations.

The new generation of workers and their children were conditioned by the boom economy; they perceived these advantages as normal. Historically they are not! Yet, now these expectations have become entitlements. Western governments have expanded social services in health, housing, and education and provided broad income-transfer programs to shelter individuals and families against economic hardship, illness, or aging. We have learned to believe that we are "entitled" to the direct allocation of resources through the political system as a supplement to the economic system.

3 *Increased educational opportunity.* Most industrialized societies have set a national goal to broaden the base in their educational system. But the slowed economy and the high unemployment rates have clearly belied the hopes raised in the hearts of students for immediate utilization of their new skills.

4 *Challenge to authority.* The uprising of youthful expectations in the late 1960s and the adoption of those expectations among workers was noted by most observers. In the United States much of the traditional radicalism of youth was intensified by a concern for the environment and a revulsion against war. This revolution in social values has continued, and the ideas originally advanced by a comparatively small number of students are now embraced by millions of young people in mainstream America.

A by-product of that upheaval has been the transformation of the attitude of young people toward authority. We have seen this change in the schools, where the young openly disagree with and challenge their teachers. It was to be expected that these changes in authority relationships would spread to the work place. Seventy percent of young workers now say that they need not take orders from a supervisor at work if they disagree. Leaders in the world of work are going to have to recognize and accept the fact that many valuable employees will not conform to traditional ways of being managed. More than ever, people are doing their own thing. Rather than resist this trend, the innovative organization is finding ways to profit from these new values. It must do a better job of matching the individual to the job, of structuring jobs to better meet the needs of the employee. I am *not* saying that we should reject performance standards or attendance requirements, nor that we should accept less than full value for the labor dollar. I am saying that, to retain competent workers, we are going to have to be more flexible in trying to meet the legitimate psychological needs that an individual brings to work. Organizations are experimenting with such solutions as part-time work, flextime, less fragmentation, more innovative control over the work itself, portable pensions, and greater educational opportunity.

5 *Decline of confidence in institutions.* In the United States the decline in respect for authority is related to a growing mistrust of institutions. Business, government, labor, the church, the military have all fallen in the general public's esteem. Mistrust in business has risen from 50 percent in 1968 to 70 percent in 1975. In fact, by 1975, nine out of ten United States citizens expressed a general mistrust of "those in power," covering business, government, and most national institutions.

Not only is public mistrust rising; so are public demands. The public is demanding of governmental agencies and of the private sector things they have not demanded before. We seem to be living in an age of increasing suspicion. As the changing context mobilizes feelings of insecurity, we seem to be more suspicious of the instititutions we blame for change. The government has always been fair game for suspicion and criticism, but these days everything that is done in the private sector seems to be suspect as well. A trend which has been partially sanctioned by such suspicion is the increasing role of government regulatory agencies—seemingly a trend toward extending control almost without end and exerting incredible pressures on all work organizations.

6 *Resistance to change.* I have noted that people dislike and fear change. Most of us, in our normal day-to-day activities, are sensitive to change; we are uncomfortable with a disruption of our established routines. Since the worker has a limited degree of control over his or her work and future, it is difficult to accept change with a sense of security. Usually, workers feel that change imposed from above is intended to meet the goals of management, to increase productivity, or to reduce costs rather than to improve working conditions or reduce stress or increase opportunity, pay, and security.

New technology does indeed often displace some in the work force. Thus, in the short term, the penalties of change may well outweigh the rewards—and this applies to workers and managers alike. Where the full-employment policy is deeply embedded, as in some companies in the United States and generally in Japan and Sweden, change is, by and large, less threatening, but this is not to say that the guarantee of a job inoculates one against reactions to change.

7   *Changing attitudes toward work.* Let us consider the question, "Does hard work always pay off?" In 1967, the majority of American students answered "yes" to this question. By 1975, 75 percent answered "no." This view of the world of work may be a realistic insight into the truth that many jobs *are* routine, dull, and boring, and do not challenge the talents of the average worker. Changing attitudes toward work, combined with the revolution in social values, have generated new interest in improving the quality of working life.

8   *The changing family.* Just as attitudes toward work are undergoing dramatic change and thus providing a different context in which stressor–stress reactions take place, so too, changes in the traditional family relationships and values provide an example of off-the-job context. Certainly, our philosophy of the family has changed. The nuclear family has by and large replaced the extended family. Traditional marriages with one man and one woman spending a lifetime together seem to be giving way to shorter-term serial marriages. The divorce rate has increased significantly. And, of extraordinary importance, marital ethics and values have changed. It has been said that we can't guarantee anything the way we used to like to believe that we could. This certainly holds true for marriage.

There is one particular change which seems to be a uniquely new phenomenon and which will be a major influence on the relationship between work life and family life. This is the dual-career family. When both partners have major responsibilities this has enormous implications for work, particularly for the problems of relocation. What happens, for instance, if a wife is offered a job in Chicago and the husband has a job in New York and both jobs pay the same amount of money and are equally gratifying? Or what happens when both work in the same city and the husband receives a fantastic offer at a great deal more money in a distant city and the wife doesn't want to go? The dual-career phenomenon is one of the greatest single factors that is going to alter the context of family life in the next twenty years.

There also exists a conflict between responsibility for career as opposed to responsibility for family. This is sometimes very real and sometimes only fancied. At times, the family serves as an excuse to avoid business commitments; at other times, presumed business needs are a handy excuse for avoiding family relationships. There appears to be an increasing acceptance of the notion that it is *all right* to put family needs ahead of business needs, to say no to a geographic transfer, for instance, even though an employer feels strongly that an employee should accept a promotional transfer to another part of the country. More than ever before, it is *all right* to adhere to one's own values, to firmly reject demands for behavior that runs contrary to them.

9 *Society is changing faster than the work place.* It is clear that change has been more rapid and penetrating in Western mores, folkways, and laws than in the work place itself. The large bureaucracies of government, industry, universities, and the military remain resistant to change. Authoritarian rules and bureaucratic practices are deeply embedded and are sheltered and seem secure from outside environment.*

We see the fabric of organizational and work life undergoing considerable change. Many other examples could be singled out, and each of the above topics could stand a great deal of elaboration. The balance of this chapter, however, will expand on a facet of the work environment that continuously affects upwards of one million workers and their families: unemployment. Regardless of the state of the economy, it is always with us. It is a potent factor in the psychosocial environment, and it contributes to a greater likelihood of reaction to a specific stressor. Many experience unemployment itself and the tedious search for new work. Many others experience the threat of job loss in a contracting organization or economy and this may be sufficient to sensitize them toward more likely reaction to a stressor.

THE THREAT OF UNEMPLOYMENT

The effects of plant closings on unemployment and subsequent re-employment were studied in two companies by Kasl and Cobb (1971). One year after plant closing the men were asked how long it took before things returned to normal. The average response indicated a subjective period of readjustment averaging four to five months. They

---

* I am deeply indebted to Jerome M. Rosow, President of Work in America Institute, for the conceptualization of some of these nine points.

said the job loss was either very disrupting or somewhat disrupting and reported suffering the most during the period of the first three months after plant closing. Their emotional difficulties clearly and significantly exceeded their financial problems during this time. Blood pressure rose progressively. Men whose symptoms stemming from job loss lasted a long time were much slower in coming down from elevated blood pressure levels than men who indicated that the discomfort did not last very long. The data on fluctuations in blood uric acid revealed a similar set of relationships. In a number of psychological areas they showed increased dissatisfaction and unhappiness as they lost their original jobs, had difficulty finding new employment, and many times subsequently lost their new jobs.

Later reports from this same study showed that the men had more illness during early periods of stressfulness than during later periods of stabilization. That is, the anticipation of job loss, the actual unemployment itself, and a period of probationary re-employment produced considerably greater ill health than was found in regularly employed men. As expected, those who described their job-loss experience as particularly severe and who were low on ego strength showed a much slower return to normal (Kasl, Gore, and Cobb, 1972).

It was clearly demonstrated that the period of *greatest* ill health is that during which *unemployment is anticipated*—the period of anticipation of the event can be more stressful than the event itself. But a strong social support system may act to moderate and reduce the influence of other variables, whether they be characteristics of the individual or of the objective experience of anticipated job loss and unemployment (Kasl, Gore, and Cobb, 1975). Chapter 7 goes into more detail on social-support systems.

THE SYMPTOMS OF UNEMPLOYMENT

Aside from the studies cited in this chapter, relatively little research has been performed relating specific illnesses to job loss or unemployment. Bourne, however, relates alcoholism in the urban black population to unemployment (1973). And suicide has been related to unemployment in both the United States and Russia. In the USSR, Petrakov (1972) associates both the incidence of suicide and the high level of mental disorder in general with chronic unemployment. In the United States it has been noted that there is a higher rate of suicide in areas characterized by many women in the work force. The same study concludes that there is a significant relationship between male unemployment and income level and suicide (Newman et al., 1973).

Severe adjustment reactions to their role change (unemployment) appear to be more difficult in those who are married and the effects may be long lasting and not completely overcome by return to work. In addition, as might be expected, those individuals who reacted severely to their unemployment experience had greater difficulty adjusting to re-employment than their colleagues. Adjustment appeared to be even more difficult for married men whose wives were able to continue their own employment (Kaufman, 1973).

Little (1973) investigated responses to unemployment among technical professionals. He found that they tend to react with self-blame, psychosomatic symptoms, depression, and irritability. Other manifestations included blaming the economic and political systems and management. Interestingly enough, the length of time of unemployment, were unrelated to these responses.

DISCUSSION

This chapter, which links disturbed behavior with unemployment in the work context, makes pessimistic reading. But the realities are clear. Unemployment and the threat of job loss are exquisitely threatening to many; seriously disrupting to others. As part of context, unemployment *does* influence psychological and physiological changes which can be measured. It *does* contribute to higher levels of ill health. And it *does* make the influence of stressors more significant.

Unemployment is also inextricably linked with a complex multitude of economic variables that are quite literally beyond the control of any individual member of society. This element of lack of control makes unemployment, for many, that much more threatening as a specter on the horizon. For millions of others, of course, it is a reality. In times of high unemployment, therefore, the context of the individual looms large in the scheme of interplay between individual vulnerability, specific stressors, and the external world.

And no longer is it just the disadvantaged, the unskilled, and the undereducated who are vulnerable. Unemployment now afflicts the professions, management, and the white-collar world as well.

Despite my seeming pessimism, there *are* ways of assisting both individuals and groups to cope with threatened and actual unemployment; with job loss and layoff. They are not magical; they are not applicable across the board; and many run counter to traditional thinking. In some instances, appropriate career counseling and preparation for jobs which *are* in demand can solve the problem. At the other extreme, the solution will require legislation to ensure full employment with major sacrifices on the part of some for the betterment of all. The simple recognition that we will continue to live in a climate of underemployment which will affect workers at all levels—and the acceptance of that fact—becomes important to all.

REFERENCES

Bourne, P. G. (1973). Alcoholism in the urban negro population. In P. G. Bourne, *Alcoholism: Progress in Research and Treatment.* New York: Academic Press, pp. 211–226.

Brenner, H. M. (1973). *Mental Illness and the Economy.* Cambridge, Mass.: Harvard University Press.

Kasl, S. V., and S. Cobb (1971). Some physical and mental health effects of job loss. *Pakistan Medical Forum* (Karachi) 6 (4): 95–106.

Kasl, S. V., S. Gore, and S. Cobb (1972). Reports of illness and illness behavior among men undergoing job loss. *Psychosomatic Medicine* **34** (5): 475.

Kasl, S. V., S. Gore, and S. Cobb (1975). The experience of losing a job: reported changes in health, symptoms and illness behavior. *Psychosomatic Medicine* **37** (2)106–122.

Kaufman, H. G. (1973). Unemployment experience among professionals. *Final Report, NIMH Grant MH-21965.*

Little, C. B. (1973). Stress responses among unemployed technical-professionals (Ph.D. Dissertation). *Dissertation Abstracts International*, Ann Arbor, Mich.: Univ. M-Films, No. 73–16750.

Newman, J. F., K. R. Whittemore, and H. G. Newman (1973). Women in the labor force and suicide. *Social Problems* **21** (2): 220–230.

Petrakov, B. D. (1972). Sociohygienic aspects of the problem of suicides and their mutual connection with mental disorders. In B. Petrakov, *Psikhicheskaya Zabolevayemost' V Nekotorykh Stranakh.* Moskva: Meditsina, pp. 248–267.

5

EVER-CHANGING INDIVIDUAL VULNERABILITY

Our vulnerability to stressful events and conditions fluctuates constantly. The ramifications of this rather commonplace notion are extraordinarily complex and have come under a great deal of scrutiny recently.

On pages 45–46 I briefly mentioned a study of stressful job changes which had apparently triggered psychiatric disorders—disorders which we might here think of as severe stress reactions. Just prior to the job change which seemed to trigger disability, the patients studied had experienced *another* stressful event. They had been able to cope with the first threat with reasonable success, but they were obviously more vulnerable to serious reaction when a threatening job change came along. It was this study which first focused my attention on the importance of individual vulnerability in determining reactions to occupational stressors and which I first reported in 1961.

The last chapter dealt with factors which are *external* to the individual, yet which are a part of an individual's life and help determine whether he or she reacts or does not react to a specific stressor. This chapter looks inward. What are some of the individual personal characteristics that seem to be associated with increased vulnerability to stressors?

Fortunately, to help us understand this increased sensitivity, we can look to recent studies which bear directly on the issue. A great deal of research, much of it highly sophisticated, has provided knowledge of the intricate processes in the brain which mediate responsiveness to stressors. Although most of those studies are beyond the scope of this book, there have been a variety of psychological and sociological reports which bear on the subject.

The impact of life events upon the individual varies as a function of the intensity and magnitude with which these events are perceived to vary from normal activity baselines, the suddenness or unpredictability with which an event occurs, or, conversely, the degree of preparedness of the individual as a result of a previous experience. For example, inability to make a monthly rent payment to a landlord has a different impact upon one who has always made such payments on time as opposed to one whose inability to do so has become a monthly routine; or, as the American television host, Johnny Carson, once put it, having a sex-change operation is traumatic enough, but discovering one has had a sex-change operation after going into surgery for a tonsillectomy is an event of life-crisis proportions (Nelson, 1974).

One's role in a particular setting, one's perception of the expectations held of him or her by others, and one's perceived ability to control or alter the situation are important factors in understanding how life events are interpreted and what reactions and coping mechanisms are evoked. For instance, how prepared was the individual for the event in question? What amount of previous experience had he or she gained from similar types of change earlier? What were the personality characteristics, the personal and cultural values, and the aspirations which might influence the way in which one interprets and copes with life changes? Attempts to evaluate the predictive value of life changes on health status at a different age and in different occupational or demographic subgroups must also be considered as one considers any one person's vulnerability at any one point in time.

To illustrate the ever-changing vulnerability of the human organism to occupational stressors in terms of specific studies, I will discuss three variables: (1) age and the aging process, (2) reactions to a buildup of many stressful events in a short time, and (3) specific personality characteristics associated with proneness to heart attack. Studies of these three variables exemplify excellent current research which is widely accepted by students of the stress phenomenon. Those with passing interest in job stress should be familiar with them.

AGES AND STAGES OF LIFE

Each stage of life has its own particular vulnerabilities and sets of coping mechanisms. The various phases of childhood and adolescence each present particular problems of coping and adaptation which the individual must meet and master. So too the young adult is still growing, maturing, learning, and adapting to the special needs of that age. And each of these periods has its special crises; its particular vulnerabilities. Most are well recognized; the psychology and psychiatry texts devote a great deal of space to the processes and problems of the formative years. Increasingly, they recognize the continued evolution of personality development in the twenties.

Less attention has been paid to the continuation of that process which goes on throughout life. Indeed, the middle adult-years of ages thirty-five to fifty-five deserve far more attention. I will use them to illustrate the particular vulnerabilities which are age related. Clinically, these problems seem to be increasingly frequent. Perhaps this is because of society's emphasis on youth; perhaps because of its high expectations for achievement. And it may be that the success oriented are the most prone to the problems of middle age often known as "the mid-life crisis."

There are many who are forty and scared stiff by their organizational roles. One of the myths of many organizations is that people who are defined by title and length of service and who are performing well are safe and secure. But much stems from the simple fact of aging. The fears of aging are incredible. The fears of being forty and over in an organization and wondering where you are going to go can be extraordinarily threatening.

By mid-life crisis or stress reaction I mean episodes of intense emotional distress, usually with depression, associated with significant changes in occupational and interpersonal values and commitments in the thirty-five to forty-five age range. Such stress reactions are not inevitable events in the middle years, though some psychiatrists tend to think they are. Most of the studies of this phenomenon have been confined to men which explains the apparent chauvinistic bias in the balance of this chapter.

"I guess I've seen a couple of thousand healthy men," says psychiatrist David Morrison, director of consultation at the Menninger Foundation, "and I haven't seen one who hasn't gone through a mid-life crisis. I don't define crisis necessarily as chaos or disaster," Dr. Morrison goes on. "But it definitely means change, that life will not be the same afterwards."

The mid-life crisis hits men without respect for occupation; it affects factory workers, schoolteachers, and psychiatrists alike. But perhaps nowhere is the mid-life crisis—and the depression usually associated with it—more evident than in the management ranks of United States corporations.

Typically, the ambitious young man in his early twenties embarks on his corporate career fantasizing his probable achievements at age forty—job, money, status. Ten or fifteen years later, however, the chasm between what he expected to achieve and what he has actually accomplished looms large. True, he may be a vice president of his company; but he is not president. He may earn a good salary and be able to afford many of the status symbols important to him; but he is not rich. And now it looks as though he will never devise the operations system that will revolutionize the industry. "The more ambitious and more creative an executive is, the more likely he i~ to suffer. The more ideas he has, the more frustrating it will be for him as he comes to realize that life is limited" (Morrison, 1975).

And thus the mid-life crisis sets in—sometimes with serious results. Everyone knows at least one talented executive in his late thirties who, after years of excellent progress up the management ladder, suddenly undergoes a radical change. He abandons his productive career for some vague, Utopian mission. Or abruptly divorces his wife of a dozen years. Or adopts a bizarre counterculture life-style. Or begins to drink heavily.

For the past several years, Yale psychologist Dr. Daniel J. Levinson has been studying the lives of forty men: ten business executives, ten blue- and white-collar workers, ten novelists, and ten biologists, all between thirty-five and forty-five years of age. Dr. Levinson has found that, regardless of their occupations and individual differences, most of the men passed through remarkably similar adult phases. Briefly, in their twenties, they went through the process of "getting into the adult world," making at least a provisional commitment to a specific career. At age thirty, they went through a minor crisis of uncertainty concerning whether they had picked the right occupation. Some changed careers at that point. From age thirty to thirty-five they went through a period of "settling down," making a definite commitment to a particular career and seeking stability and control. (An executive, for example, might set the specific goal of earning $50,000 a year by the time he is forty.) Then, at the age of thirty-five, they entered a delicate phase of "becoming one's own man." For men in this stage, it is no longer satisfying simply to be a rising middle-level executive; they want autonomy and feel frustrated at not being allowed to make enough of their own decisions.

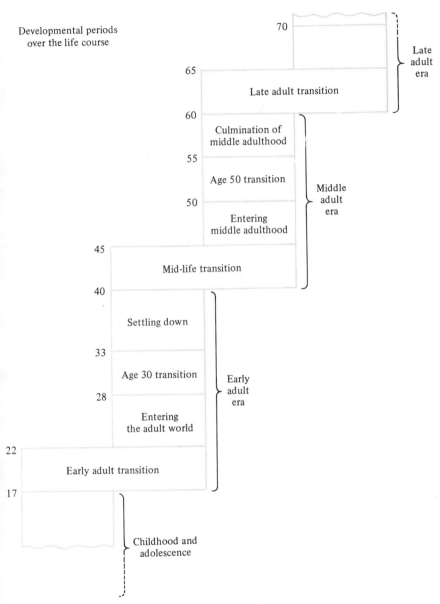

FIG. 5.1 *The seasons of a man's life. (From* The Seasons of a Man's Life, *by Daniel J. Levinson. Copyright © 1978 by Daniel J. Levinson. Reprinted by permission of Alfred A. Knopf, Inc.)*

Dr. Levinson calls ages thirty-nine to forty-two the "mid-life transition period." At this point the executive desperately needs a clear, strong signal of approval from his employer. But even if he gets a promotion, he is still dissatisfied; his achievements seem hollow.

As a man approaches forty he begins to feel at least some of the physical effects of aging. His hair thins, he needs glasses, he no longer finds it easy to lose that fifteen pounds. He may also experience a decline in sexual activity; significantly, it is in their late thirties that many men first become attracted to much younger women, as though twenty-year-olds had magical powers to stave off old age.

Most men, even the over achievers, survive the mid-life crisis undamaged. But a few do develop serious stress reactions, frequently by withdrawing into a form of psychological retirement in which they function at only a minimal level. Because they are likely to have achieved a position of responsibility by age forty, their lackluster performance and abandonment of leadership can have a corrosive effect on those who work for and with them.

Few would blame such reaction on a mid-life crisis alone. But it seems to be a period of particular vulnerability, a time of low resistance when a combination of other forces, internal and external, can torment a person in a way that would not have bothered that individual when younger.

At forty-one Amos McPherson had become his own person but he was ripe for mid-life transition. Indeed, as he thought to himself, everything was going *too* well! He had, for two years, had staff responsibility for a major company function in the suburban headquarters of a large manufacturer. He had autonomy, the respect of his colleagues and superiors, and a substantial salary and stock-option plan. He and his family felt that their life was stable, secure. His sons, ages fifteen and thirteen, were doing well in school. His wife enjoyed a comfortable routine with part-time work as an editor and an active social and cultural life.

Yet the "impossible" happened. McPherson's company merged with one of equal size. Duplicate staff functions were eliminated in the successor organization and McPherson was out—overnight, unexpectedly.

His new assignment was to a line position at a regional headquarters in a nearby city. It was "the only thing open." While his salary was not reduced, the new job was far inferior to the the previous job in status and pay level. McPherson knew he would be lucky to receive cost-of-living increases for the foreseeable future. Thus, the signals he got from his employer were clear and strong, but they were not the signals of approval that Dr. Levenson suggests are so necessary at this age.

After a period of overtly expressed anger, McPherson became depressed. While he was not seriously disabled, he did have symptoms of irritability, frustration, insomnia, and, increasingly, bowel and stomach disorders. His new job required a long commute and left much less time for his family and avocational interests and it stimulated a searching evaluation of his occupational goals. This reassessment, however, led only to increasing frustration. He blamed himself for not seeing the *potential* threat and not getting his "ducks lined up" outside in order to step into a higher rather than lower job level with another organization. He felt locked into his present job; that he was not in a position to look elsewhere "because I couldn't really sell myself now."

These same seeds of self-doubt permeated all aspects of his life. He questioned the future viability of his marriage, which did indeed begin to founder leading to eventual separation and divorce.

Amos McPherson's experience was not unique. At his age, he was ripe for a transition and was particularly vulnerable to the potent stressor of what he regarded as a demeaning job change. His stress reaction was a predictable response.

Although it would have been advisable, McPherson did not obtain professional help but resigned himself to "sticking it out." He gave the job less time and attention than it deserved, gradually turning his attention to outside interests. Over the next few years, with the growth of the new company, he found his job responsibilities enlarged and, with very little effort on his part, regained occupational status and responsibility approximating those he had lost. By middle adulthood he was able to be more objective about the job-loss experience and developed a quiet contentment that he had weathered the storm—albeit with the sacrifice of what he had earlier seen as several potentially satisfying years.

One may look at many aspects of today's society for additional explanations of heightened mid-life susceptibility to stressors. To take one example, our culture no longer provides the social support that was given in the past by the extended family. Thus when youngsters leave home for college or work, "the empty-nest syndrome" requires adjustments at home which are often difficult. Parents, without the needs and distractions of children at home are faced with the need to develop new interests, activities, and relationships. The pressures faced during these years frequently lead to divorce. But divorce itself brings about its own special vulnerabilities and needs for adaptation. Many women return to the work force or enter it for the first time as part of their mid-life experience. This too calls for new life-styles and presents many with very specific vulnerability to stressors. Finally, the women's movement has successfully promoted greater equality between the sexes. For those reared in the more traditional society of male domination, the heightened consciousness of new role differentiation may stimulate feelings of unrest and a questioning of old attitudes and activities.

What can a person caught up in a mid-life stress reaction do beyond seeking professional counsel? One possibility is to reduce one's aspirations. This is not easy, but it can be done if approached in small steps over several years, gradually accommodating oneself to a new self-image. For many this is an automatic process as the continuing adjustment to changing reality dictates. For others it requires a deliberate and conscious planning effort and professional assistance.

Another response to the mid-life crisis is renewed effort with an increased commitment to make full use of time remaining. Both of these responses center on the occupational arena in persons for whom job achievement has been an important source of self-esteem. But sometimes the solution lies in other directions: The arena of principal concern may shift from occupational to interpersonal commitments.

As Drs. David and Beatrix Hamburg point out, a special new relationship may be formed under the stimulus of mid-life doubts and concerns. This relationship may be a deep friendship, a love affair, or a new marriage. It may be seen as an alternative source of satisfaction, replacing a prior emphasis on occupational satisfaction and providing a vital new basis for self-esteem. Or, on the other hand, it may be viewed as facilitating renewed occupational efforts, providing a new stimulus, encouragement, assistance, and even inspiration.

Such a relationship may have many other connotations. It may relieve old burdens; it may add new satisfactions; it may provide a sense of recapturing youth. It may open new vistas—information, ideas, shared experiences. The person in mid-life may find that he or she has fewer inhibitions than in youth, less uncertainty, and more confidence in taking advantage of new opportunities. Self-esteem may be renewed by the fact that the individual has been able to earn the respect of someone to whom special value is now attached. Old assets may now elicit new responses—a storehouse of past experiences, skills, and knowledge can now be shared with a new person. The relationship may be felt as a kind of special accomplishment. It may elicit favorable reactions from others. It may be experienced as invigorating—sexually, occupationally, and in other ways.

In these middle-adult years, some seek new gratifications in the interpersonal sphere while holding occupational commitment essentially constant. Others seek new gratification in the occupational sphere while holding interpersonal commitments essentially the same. Some make major changes in both arenas.

> As the years pass physical vigor counts for less, knowledge and judgment more; grand exploits less, integrity more; technical skills less, compassion more. And always, even in the drastically changed context of the modern world, satisfaction depends on the network of enduring and dependable human relationships that has been at the heart of human evolution for millions of years.
>
> (HAMBURG AND HAMBURG, 1979)

LIFE CHANGE AND VULNERABILITY

Although we generally think of changes in life as being frequently stressful in and of themselves, it has been demonstrated that the occurrence of several important changes at once may contribute to increased individual vulnerability to illness. As a result of the development of a method of tabulating and quantifying life changes, researchers have been enabled to investigate systematically whether people who have experienced more numerous and/or serious recent change might be more vulnerable to illness. The underlying assumption is that when people's lives are in a relatively steady state of psychosocial adjustment with few life changes, less illness will be found and, conversely, that when a great many serious recent changes have taken place, subsequent ill health may be expected.

The work of Drs. Thomas Holmes and Richard Rahe at the University of Washington in the mid-sixties is usually considered the seminal effort to measure life events (Holmes and Rahe, 1967). Actually, their work evolved from that of the distinguished psychiatric leader Professor Adolph Meyer of Johns Hopkins, who developed the concept of a life chart to demonstrate vividly the influence of life events on adaptation in the study of individual psychiatric patients.

Holmes and Rahe's initial work involved the construction of a Schedule of Recent Events (SRE) questionnaire to document in a systematic way life events reported by research subjects during the years prior to developing illnesses. The SRE included a broad spectrum of recent life changes, including personal, social, occupational, and family life adjustment.

The forty-three life-change questions contained in the SRE were scaled, and each was assigned a numerical value. This was done by asking 400 people of both sexes and of different ages, races, religions, educational backgrounds, etc., to consider one of the life-change events, marriage, as having an arbitrary value of 500. The individuals were then instructed to assign a Life-Change-Unit (LCU) value for the remaining life-change events, using marriage as the reference point. For example, when the subjects evaluated a life-change event such as a change in residence, they were to ask themselves, "Is a change in residence more, less, or perhaps equal to the amount of change and adjustment involved in marriage?" If the subject decided that it was more, he or she was to indicate how much more by choosing a proportionately larger LCU value than the 500 assigned to marriage. If it was less, he or she would choose a proportionately smaller number than 500. This process was repeated for each of the life-change events in the SRE questionnaire. Among the research subjects there was remarkable agreement on values. Table 5–1 shows the categories and the original Seattle values.

Once these LCU weightings were established, researchers could assign to recent life-change events values reflecting the average degree of intensity of life change. Arbitrary time intervals were selected over which life changes were summed in order to compute incidence rates. This was done for two years, one year, six months, and three months.

Their findings indicated that there was an increase in the research subjects' LCU values during the year or two prior to illnesses. The observed buildup in the subjects' LCU scores did not seem to be related to the *type* of illness, but a positive relationship was found between the LCU score during the year prior to illness and the *severity* of the subsequent illness.

In a later study the majority of subjects who recorded a total of 150 LCU or less in the preceding year reported good health for the

TABLE 5.1 *The Holmes-Rahe Schedule of Recent Life Events*

Rank	Event	Value
1	Death of spouse	100
2	Divorce	73
3	Marital separation	65
4	Jail term	63
5	Death of close family member	63
6	Personal injury or illness	53
7	Marriage	50
8	Fired from work	47
9	Marital reconciliation	45
10	Retirement	45
11	Change in family member's health	44
12	Pregnancy	40
13	Sex difficulties	39
14	Addition to family	39
15	Business readjustment	39
16	Change in financial status	38
17	Death of close friend	37
18	Change to different line of work	36
19	Change in number of marital arguments	35
20	Mortgage or loan over $10,000	31
21	Foreclosure of mortgage or loan	30
22	Change in work responsibilities	29
23	Son or daughter leaving home	29
24	Trouble with in-laws	29
25	Outstanding personal achievement	28
26	Spouse begins or stops work	26
27	Starting or finishing school	26
28	Change in living conditions	25
29	Revision of personal habits	24
30	Trouble with boss	23
31	Change in work hours, conditions	20
32	Change in residence	20
33	Change in schools	20
34	Change in recreational habits	19
35	Change in church activities	19
36	Change in social activities	18
37	Mortgage or loan under $10,000	17
38	Change in sleeping habits	16
39	Change in number of family gatherings	15
40	Change in eating habits	15
41	Vacation	13
42	Christmas season	12
43	Minor violation of the law	11

following year. When yearly LCU values ranged between 150 and 300, an illness was reported during the following year in about half the cases. Among the relatively few subjects who registered more than 300 LCU per year, an illness was recorded during the following year in 70 percent of cases.

In the last fifteen years Holmes, Rahe and many colleagues have used the concept of life-change units as useful predictors of susceptibility to subsequent illness. The approach has held up remarkably well in a wide range of samples of people from several countries and cultures.

One might logically speculate, too, that the higher the numerical equivalent of LCUs, the greater the susceptibility an individual will have to a stressful event on the job (or off the job, for that matter). To date, I know of no such study, but it *would* be interesting to remove the LCU items which relate to work from the scale and to see if an accumulation of a high score on non-work-related items might have some predictive powers when it comes to reacting to "job stress."

PERSONALITY AND HEART ATTACK

As a final example of characteristics associated with proneness to stress reactions, the work of two San Francisco cardiologists deserves special attention. Some twenty-five years ago Drs. Meyer Friedman and Ray Rosenman began their investigation into the relationship between personality characteristics and the likelihood of heart attack. Informal observations of their coronary patients suggested they were likely to be competitive strivers rather than placid, more docile people. From Friedman and Rosenman's subsequent research, we now have fairly well documented evidence that aggresive achievers, whom they described as having "Type A" behavior, are more vulnerable to heart attack than those at the opposite end of the personality spectrum, "Type B".

In 1960 they embarked on a massive study to determine personality variables which might be associated with the likelihood of heart disease. Their work lasted for ten years and involved 35,000 men between the ages of thirty-one and fifty-nine, each of whom was given a behavioral classification based on interviews and/or observations. None had any prior record of heart disease. By 1970, 257 had developed coronary heart disease, and 70 percent of the victims were what the cardiologists had categorized as Type A (Friedman and Rosenman, 1974).

Friedman and Rosenman call Type A behavior an action-emotion complex that can be observed in any person who is *aggressively* involved in a *chronic, incessant* struggle to achieve more and more in less and less time, and if required to do so, against the opposing efforts of other things or other persons.

The Type B person, on the other hand, is rarely harried by desires to obtain a wildly increasing number of things or participate in an endlessly growing series of events in an ever decreasing amount of time. The Type A individual is extremely competitive, constantly tending to challenge others—in sports, at work, and even in casual discussions. Type A people characteristically overreact and generally are hypercritical—both of themselves (to themselves) and of others (more openly). They might fume at something a Type B person would brush off as inconsequential.

Type A's are said to have a great sense of urgency concerning time. They tend to thrive on deadlines and create them if none exist. Similarly, they establish difficult goals if none are set for them, and are quick to become impatient when goals and deadlines are not achieved. In contrast, Type B's are more contemplative. They take the time to ponder alternatives and usually feel there is plenty of time.

A's tend to be more status oriented and are known for their struggles for recognition and achievement. Outwardly confident and self-assured, their underlying insecurity is often plainly evident to their intimates. Nor are they ever satisfied with the symbols of achieved status; they constantly, restlessly hunger for more.

Friedman and Rosenman concluded that in the absence of Type A Behavior Pattern, coronary heart disease almost never occurs before seventy years of age, regardless of the fatty foods eaten, the cigarettes smoked, or the lack of exercise. But when this behavior pattern is present, coronary heart disease can easily erupt in one's thirties or forties.

They also found that Type A's were not only three times more likely to develop heart disease than Type B's, but that A's who were low on other coronary-risk factors were still more heart-disease prone than B's who smoked, were hypertensive, and whose family histories included heart attacks.

Neat categories such as Friedman and Rosenman's are always over-simplifications. They represent extremes. More important, they are but statistical correlations. Many Type B's *do* get coronary heart disease; many A's do not. And B's and A's are at the opposite ends of a continuum; the majority are toward its center.

Nevertheless considerable research is accumulating which supports the relationship between Type A behavior and vulnerability to heart attack. A sociologist, Dr. Walter Wardwell at the University of Connecticut, compared men who had coronary heart disease with those who did not. His findings not only provided support for Friedman and Rosenman's contention, but went further to suggest a specific reason for the correlation. "The core element (in Type A behavior) may simply be . . . the proclivity on the part of some people in contradistinction to others to translate psychological and situational tensions, conflicts, and frustrations into bodily symptoms. The variety of ways in which such stresses are expressed appear to include restless activity, ambitious strivings, bodily symptoms of many different sorts, and pathogenic atherosclerotic and thrombotic processes" (Wardwell, 1973, p. 531).

While research reports continue to grow in number in support of the Type A-Type B relationship to heart attack, sound research of a different sort puts the issue in a different perspective. Dr. Lawrence Hinkle, Jr., Director of Human Ecology at New York Hospital-Cornell Medical Center, carried out an exhaustive study of 260,000 career employees of the Bell System. He divided the men into two groups—those who were hired without having college degrees and those who came to the company with college degrees. The former were generally of blue-collar background; the latter were children of parents who were managers, owners of small businesses and salaried white-collar workers.

In the beginning of 1962, Hinkle and his colleagues followed these groups prospectively for five years and investigated each death and every disabling event of coronary heart disease that occured among them. They observed almost 2,000 deaths and 4,000 disabling "coronary events."

From their study it became evident that, in this population, coronary heart disease is more a disease of the blue-collar workmen and foremen than of white-collar managers and executives. It was, as might be expected, the college graduates who moved into management—and they were, presumably, a group more apt to express Type A behavior. Hinkle comments, "I call your attention to the fact that men who move rapidly up the managerial ladder and become managers early in their careers have no excess of coronary heart disease in spite of their rapid upward social mobility" (Hinkle, 1973).

Friedman and Rosenman are aware that research to date has only uncovered a *correlation* between behavior patterns and heart disease. It has not established that such behavior *causes* heart disease or that a change in behavior patterns can prevent attacks.* They are now working on a study to determine if behavior changes can help prevent future heart attacks in people who have already had one. One thing is clear: Severe Type A behavior is one of several coronary-risk factors.

COMMENT

A person is said to be vulnerable when he or she is open to attack or damage or capable of being wounded. Personal vulnerability is a key determinant in the complex equation which may conclude with an occupational stress reaction—and it is often elusive. In any given person, clinical investigation will usually uncover the degree to which individual vulnerability in a stressful situation is significant. In *groups* at risk, it is not quite so simple. (Not that a clinical evaluation is all that easy!) Different ages and stages in life present uniquely different susceptibilities to stressors. Yet many people sail through most potentially stressful times without serious reaction. Recent work, such as that of Levinson, clearly pinpoints the most *likely* adult periods of stress and, more important, gives us insight as to why. Most adult males experience a mid-life crisis. But some are extraordinarily minor in nature. The frame of reference presented here is helpful both in understanding vulnerabilities of specific ages and in considering coping strategies. But greatly enhanced susceptibility to job stress is *not* inevitable between ages forty and fifty. More likely, yes. Inevitable, no.

Holmes and Rahe's life-change units are similarly useful—but inconclusive. A recent buildup of major changes *does* tend to make the average person more vulnerable to subsequent illness. But other research suggests that if one can retain most of the threads of one's customary interests, affiliations, and activities during a stressful period, the likelihood of adverse reaction is sharply reduced.

It is also true that the aggressive, assertive, competitive Type A person *is* statistically more vulnerable to heart attack, but here, too,

---

* See Chapter 6 for discussion of the faults of conclusions based solely on correlational analyses.

one must not self-diagnose one's self into hypochondriacal antici-pation of early coronary death if one identifies with that model.

Awareness of our ever-changing susceptibility to stressors is important and useful in understanding our own and others' reactions. But *identifying* with data that is only statistically significant for masses of people with certain similar characteristics is, at best, unwise!

REFERENCES

Brown, G. W., M. N. Bhrolchain, and T. Harris (1975). Social class and psychiatric disturbance among women in an urban population. *Sociology* 9:225–254.

Friedman, M., and R. H. Rosenman (1974). *Type A: Your Behavior and Your Heart.* New York: Knopf.

Hamburg, D. A., and B. A. Hamburg (1979). Stress and coping in mid-life. In L. Levi (ed.), *Society, Stress and Disease—Working Life.* New York: Oxford University Press.

Hinkle, Lawrence E., Jr. (1973). Coronary heart disease and sudden death in actively employed American men. *Bulletin of the New York Academy of Medicine* 49 (6): 467–474.

Holmes, T. H., and R. H. Rahe (1967). Social readjustment rating scale. *Journal of Psychosomatic Research* 11:213.

Levinson, D. J., C. D. Darrow, E. B. Klein, M. H. Levinson, and B. Mckee (1978).*The Seasons of Man's Life.* New York: Knopf.

McLean, A. A. (1961). Medical problems in employment continuity of senior citizens. *New York State Journal of Medicine* 61 (17): 2901–2905.

Morrison, David (1975). Executives and the mid-life crisis. *Dun's Review,* June, p. 48.

Nelson, P. D. (1974). Comment. In E. K. E. Gunderson and R. H. Rahe, *Life Stress and Illness.* Springfield: Charles C. Thomas, p. 79.

Wardwell, Walter I. (1973). A study of stress and coronary heart disease in an urban population. *Bulletin of the New York Academy of Medicine* 49 (6): 521–531.

6

STRESSFUL EVENTS AND CONDITIONS AT WORK

Research into stressors at work bears out the notion that literally anything can be termed stressful if the individual's vulnerability is extraordinarily high and if a supportive environment is unavailable. Consider the following:

- Particular *occupations* have been associated with greater risk of ulcers, coronary heart disease, and purely psychiatric disability—but the same association can be made between these illnesses and social class and specific ages.

- Shift work is associated with job dissatisfaction and higher levels of anxiety and other measures of stress reaction—but so is work which does not allow the individual to participate in decisions about the work process.

- Being evaluated—a customary part of every job—is said to be a stressor—but so are both excessive workload and insufficient workload.

- Changes at work are stressful—but so is monotony.

- Ambiguous and conflictful work is associated with stress reactions—but job loss is even more stressful.

In Chapter 3, I suggested that change is a common denominator for events that are perceived as particularly stressful. In the case of stressful *events*, I believe we will find this to be the case. But there are, as well, *conditions* associated with disorders found in people who are "under stress" where change is *not* a necessary factor. This chapter is organized around (1) stressful events involving change and, (2) stable conditions which are commonly threatening to people on the job but which do not involve change.

EVENTS

We accept resistance to change as a fact of life. We expect bureaucrats to be defensive when challenged by innovators and isolated, rural townspeople to be suspicious of new techniques. We take it for granted that the loss of loved ones is deeply distressing.

The pace of change in today's society is rapidly accelerating. Indeed, according to some, the rapidity of change is undermining the stability both of society and of work organizations. Futurist Donald Schon of M.I.T. points out that we are living in a time of loss of the stable state; stable views of occupational, religious, organizational, and value systems have been eroded. In *Beyond the Stable State* (1972), he demonstrates how established institutions normally respond to change with what he terms "dynamic conservatism": They fight to remain the same.

Both the individual and the organization have built-in resistance to change and stressful events are often those that *require* change in both the individual and the organization.

Changes which are stressful at work often involve loss. The loss may be minor, like giving up comfortable techniques when the work process changes. Or it may involve an irreversible destruction of social bonds, as when an esteemed supervisor leaves and one whose qualities are unknown comes on the scene. Loss may involve moving from a supportive work group to a competitive, hostile one. Or a worker may lose self-esteem if he or she is unable to perform a new and complicated routine. Certainly the ultimate occupational stress— the loss of one's job (see Chapter 4)—can produce a serious grief reaction.

While some specific stressors on the job may lead to grief or to melancholia and depression, most do not. Rather, they call into play a variety of coping mechanisms which are generally healthy and constructive and help the individual to arrive at a new plateau of adjustment to his or her work world in a reasonably short time.

Regardless of whether the loss is "real" or purely a perceived threat to one's psychic well-being, the reactions are apt to be the same. The grief reaction may be brief and scarcely noticed or it may lead to a very real sense of bereavement. In the latter case—and, fortunately, it is rare—there will be emotional pain, often feelings of depression. Usually the individual will exhibit physical reactions, which include feelings of weakness and emptiness, exhaustion, decreased appetite, and insomnia. Anxiety and tension may also be prominent symptoms, as well as agitation and restlessness, hand wringing, and an appearance of confusion and puzzlement.

A normal grief reaction is worked through and resolved fairly soon. The expression of grief is a signal to others; it often draws support and may lead to the formation of new bonds. But the mourning process which helps a person work through the reaction to the loss of a loved person or the loss of an abstraction such as a skill or application of expertise is not always successful. As Freud pointed out, melancholia (or serious depressive illness) instead of grief may subsequently develop.

In other words, there may be a wide range of reaction to any loss at work (or elsewhere in one's life) up to and including serious, incapacitating withdrawal and avoidance with physical and psychological symptoms and even a sense of complete worthlessness.

Stressful events

Examples of stressful events that trigger fairly serious reaction were given in Chapter 1. Here I will discuss examples of some relatively common *categories* of threatening or stressful events.

Evaluation. Evaluation is a stressful event that is nearly universal in the world of work; it is a built-in part of the work structure. Evaluation serves as both an opportunity and a barrier to advancement. It is always a test of one's adequacy compared with others. Work organizations are, of course, competitive societies, and this threatening element of competition and examination is a part of our lives from a very early age. Marked anxiety about examinations is commonplace. In fact, examination anxiety is so widespread and serious in the school setting that it has attracted the attention of a number of major research programs. Most such studies reveal the distress experienced by many of those anticipating upcoming examinations and the severe psychosomatic and behavioral disturbances associated with apprehension.

Of course not all individuals are equally vulnerable to the potential stresses of evaluation. Understanding the personality characteristics which help to explain this is important. Some individuals are not greatly disturbed by evaluation because their definition of themselves as persons is one of great confidence or is otherwise out of keeping with the terms of the evaluation. Some people have strong needs to achieve or to be positively regarded and others have few such needs. Some are fragile in the face of stress of evaluation and react to even the possibility of evaluation with marked apprehension and with doubts about their ability to meet their own or some other's standards.*

Some people have good social support systems, some do not. For instance, some are intensely pressured by friends and relatives to achieve at a standard beyond their ability, whereas others obtain support, acceptance, and understanding of their level of competence. And evaluation *situations* differ as well, some being particularly destructive and punitive, while others are more supportive and less threatening or damaging to the person's self-esteem. For some the work setting is almost constantly threatening because of its evaluative implications while for others evaluation is a negligible source of psychological stress.

Individual vs. organizational practices. Institutional practices which are in conflict with a person's standards, values, and mores sometimes lead to events that are quite stressful for the employee. What of the employer who requires an employee to contribute to a political institution which he or she cannot abide? What of the sales person asked to "push" a company product which he or she knows to be grossly inferior to a competitor's? Or the employee asked to bribe a public official to close a profitable contract? Or the more subtle conflict when an employee discovers his or her employer to be quietly engaged in other forms of dishonest or marginal practice in conflict with both the stated values of the corporate charter and much against the individual values of the person?

There are probably many instances in the daily work setting in which a person is called upon to take part in activities which violate

---

* For this concept I am indebted to Dr. Richard Lazarus of U.C.L.A.

standards of conduct that are important to him or to her. In such persons considerable anxiety can be produced by the conflict between institutional practices and personal values.

It is easy to say that such a person should give up his or her job, but this is a solution which may create its own economic and social stressors. For most people, the personal values involved may not be important enough for this to be a serious problem and, besides, with a little bit of mental gymnastics, including rationalization and denial, the issue (in minor cases) tends to fade away.

The corporate charter. An awareness of institutional practices and policies that block important modes of individual coping is crucial in understanding stress reactions. Since individuals vary greatly in the kinds of coping mechanisms they find useful, any institutional pattern that blocks the use of such forms of coping will increase the stress reaction for that individual.

Consider the shy and introverted person who has difficulties in social situations but who is pressured by management practices or institutional custom to participate in frequent social functions. Organizational practices often interfere with the individual's idiosyncratic ways of coping and thus increase the number of stress reactions by impairing the individual's ability to manage his or her life effectively with the coping devices upon which he or she depends.

Hans Selye comments that "among people engaged in the most common occupation of modern society—the lower and middle echelons of business, industry, agriculture, and public life, from the simple handyman to the administrator or public servant with limited responsibilities—one of the major sources of distress arises from dissatisfaction with life, namely, from disrespect for their own accomplishments. As they grow older and progress toward the completion of their career, they tend to doubt the importance of their achievements. They are frustrated by the conviction that they really could have done, and would have liked to do, much more. These people often spend the rest of their lives in search of scapegoats, grumbling about the lack of opportunity, excessive responsibilities toward their relatives—anything will do to avoid the most painful confession: that the fault was really their own" (Selye, 1974).

Aging and retirement. The prospects of aging and retirement confront the person with a struggle between engagement and disengagement in the life process that work represents. Disengagement threatens the person with loss of independence and significance. The problem is often anticipated long before it happens, and the gradual movement toward this period of life and impending loss of one's potency and productivity is signaled in many ways—by peers, management, or one's own sense of the inability to function as well as one previously did. As with all other psychosocial sources of stress, this one may have its most poignant expression on the job. The particular vulnerabilities of aging were discussed in more detail in Chapter 5.

CONDITIONS

Sometimes the work environment causes stress even though there has been no significant change. Social psychologists have studied these relatively stable conditions associated with stressful work using measurements of attitude and job satisfaction together with self-reports of work pressures. They have made many correlations based on measurements of reactions to stress—both psychological and physical. But relatively little sound research exists that relates working *conditions* to physical or psychiatric disorder. In other words, there is very little *medical* support for psychologists' conclusions that working conditions which lead to job dissatisfaction and stressfulness *cause* disability. There remains a glaring need for research in this area.

Most of the studies conducted by behavioral scientists (as opposed to medical investigators) rely heavily on the use of correlation for their conclusions. The simple (and sometimes not so simple) comparison of one factor with another provides, as we will see, some dramatic conclusions about the relationship between stressful work and undesirable personal situations. But many of the studies make inferences about causality which cannot be accepted at face value. The fact that two conditions are correlated does *not* mean that one causes the other. Correlation analysis fails to point out the role of intervening variables—those many events and conditions in a causal chain between those factors which do eventually correlate. A causal chain is not necessarily only two variables long, although many of these studies might have us believe that it is.

Another difficulty with this research lies in the use of the term "stress." The word is used sometimes to denote stressful events, sometimes to denote the effect of these events on work performance, and sometimes to denote an individual's reaction in terms of disordered health. These differences show up in research results as well. Often they simply are not comparable.

I find other problems as well. Some researchers attempt to generalize from a comprehensive study of a very small but highly specific sample. Others draw their conclusions from large samples but use quite simplistic survey techniques. Some use control groups; others do not. Clearly, it is important to understand the methodology employed before accepting the results—or the significance of the results—of any study.

Stressful occupations

The stressfulness of particular occupations has been debated for many years. The conclusions about the psychologically stressful component of an occupation which might lead to a worker's physical and mental disability have been based largely on educated guesses and, to some degree, researcher bias. Air-traffic controllers, physicians, assembly-line workers, and the policemen, for example, all are supposed to work in particularly stressful circumstances.

Because of publicity concerning the various stressors associated with these jobs, Michael Smith, Michael Colligan, Richard Horning, and Joseph Hurrell (1978) of the Behavioral Factors Branch of The National Institute for Occupational Safety and Health have noted that, "No objective criteria presently exist which would permit a comparison of these occupations with other job classifications in terms of inherent psychological job stress factors and/or their resultant health impact. It is therefore possible that other common, less publicized occupations expose workers to equivalent, or even more, psychological job stressors and health/strain consequences."

As one step in helping to clarify these muddy waters, they examined the specific occupations of patients admitted to mental hospitals. This involved an epidemiological examination of mental health center records to determine the frequency of admission of individuals employed in major occupational categories. These frequencies were then related to population norms for each job classification (based on census data) to give an occupational incidence rate of mental disorders. The study utilized over 22,000 health records of stress-related disorders for workers in Tennessee taken from three separate data sources. Occupational differences in the incidence of stress-related disorders were determined for 130 occupations. Occupations and groups of occupations were compared. Results indicated that general and construction laborers, secretaries, inspectors, clinical laboratory technicians, office managers, managers/administrators, foremen, waitresses/waiters, operatives, mine operatives, farm workers, and painters all showed an incidence of stress-related disease significantly greater than expected.

They also found that occupational *status level* has no relationship to the incidence of stress-related disease. Both white- and blue-collar employees showed high *and* low incidence of stress-related disease. Managers, foremen, and shop-floor employees all showed high and low incidence; skilled and unskilled workers also showed both high and low incidence.

While the results were confusing, the evidence that construction laborers had the highest incidence of stress-related disease is congruent with a number of previous research conclusions that the lower ends of the socioeconomic continuum are more prone to stress reactions than those in the middle or upper class.

Assembly lines. Many cite the assembly line as being particularly stressful because of its fragmentation of work and the lack of worker participation in decisions about the work process. It is increasingly evident that physical and mental health is adversely affected by repetitive work and "dehumanizing" work environments. A study of 150 men with evidence of early coronary heart disease in a population of over 4,000 industrial workers in Berlin reported that more of these individuals were employed in industries using assembly-line systems than in any other work technology. In a study of the automobile industry, Kornhauser (1965) found that "poor mental health" was directly related to unpleasant working conditions and the necessity to work rapidly and to expend a lot of physical effort. He also noted that the lower the status of the job, the greater the prevalence of mental disorder as defined by his tests and questionnaires.

Piecework. A psychologically close cousin to assembly work is piecework. It too has been indicted as stressful, particularly by researchers in Sweden. Both laboratory and field studies have shown piecework to be associated with increased numbers of accidents and higher levels of conditions associated with stressfulness. Interestingly, practical experiments have shown that these measurements fall back to normal levels when such workers are placed on fixed monthly salaries. Admittedly, productivity is higher under piece-rate systems than under salaried conditions, but the wear and tear on employees brings into serious question the value of such a system under ordinary circumstances.

Cary Cooper and Judi Marshall at the Department of Management Sciences at the University of Manchester conceive of five categories of conditions which are not associated with any one specific occupation but which researchers have deemed stressful. I will follow their systemic view of environmental stressors at work in the balance of this section. For anyone interested in more detail, their summary of the literature relating occupational stress to both coronary heart disease and mental health is well worth reading. They list factors intrinsic to a particular job, role in the organization, career development, relationships at work, and just "being" in an organization (Cooper and Marshall, 1976).

Factors intrinsic to a job

Although many characteristics of a particular task can be stressful, let me illustrate this category with what John French and Robert Caplan speak of as quantitative and qualitative overload. Quantitative means simply having too much to do; qualitative means that the work is simply too difficult. (The complementary phenomena of quantitative and qualitative underload have also been suggested as potential sources of stress as illustrated by the work of both Lennart Levi and Clinton Weiman discussed on pages 4 and 5 respectively).

The pressure of having too much to do or at least feeling that one has too much to do would seem to be a fairly obvious stressor. A study of one hundred young coronary patients found that 25 percent of them had been working at two jobs and an additional 45 percent had jobs that required them to put in sixty or more hours each week (Russek and Zohman, 1958). Although prolonged emotional strain preceded the attack in 91 percent of the cases, similar stress was observed in only 20 percent of the control subjects. Another study also reported findings which support a relationship between hours of work and death from coronary heart disease (Breslau and Buell, 1960). In this study, workers in light industry under the age of forty-five who were on the job more than forty-eight hours a week had twice the risk of death from such illness compared with similar workers working forty hours or less.

Another investigation on quantitative overload involved a representative national sample of 1,496 workers. It found that overload was significantly related to a number of indicators of stress reaction: excessive drinking, low motivation to work, low self-esteem, and absenteeism (Margolis et al., 1974).

John French and his colleagues (1965) studied 122 university administrators and professors to learn the effects of qualitative overload on health. They found that there was no significant correlation between qualitative overload and low self-esteem in the administrators but there was a significant correlation for the professors. The greater the quality of work expected of the professor, the lower his or her self-esteem. Several other studies have reported an association between qualitative work overload and level of blood cholesterol (high cholesterol levels are commonly associated with coronary heart disease). There was also a correlation between tax deadlines for accountants and medical students performing an examination under observation and illness.

In reviewing the intrinsic factors of a job which seem to be associated with stressful conditions in this research, one must again keep in mind the tremendous importance of the other factors in our overlapping circles—individual vulnerability and the overall environment in which one functions. Work overload must not be viewed in isolation but must be seen relative to the individual's personality. Further, since qualitative and quantitative overload measures stem from the perceptions of the individual, they may be influenced by that individual's predilections and personality predispositions.

Role in organization

The nature of one's role in a work organization often underlies stress reactions. A great deal of research has focused on role ambiguity and role conflict. Ambiguity exists when an individual has insufficient information about his or her work role—where there is uncertainty concerning the scope and responsibilities of the job and uncertainty about what coworkers expect. Individuals who suffer from role ambiguity have been found to experience low job satisfaction, high job-related tension, and low self-confidence. Increased blood pressure and pulse rate have also been associated with role ambiguity, as have depression and reported intention to quit a job.

Role conflict exists when an individual in a particular work role is torn by conflicting job demands or doing things that he or she does not really want to do or does not think are part of the job. An example of this would be when a person is caught between two groups each of which has differing expectations of the role occupant. Role conflict has been related to low job satisfaction and high job-related tension. French and Caplan (1970) telemetered the heart rates of twenty-two men for a two-hour period while the men were at work in their offices. They found that the individual's heart rate was strongly related to his report of role conflict.

Much of the work studying role conflict and ambiguity has originated at the Institute for Social Research at the University of Michigan. The above findings come from studies by Robert Kahn, John French, and Robert Caplan, who are among Michigan's best-known role theorists.

Several studies identify another potential stressor associated with one's organizational role: responsibility for people. There is a difference between responsibility for people and responsibility for things (such as equipment and budgets). Higher responsibility for people frequently means that one has to spend more time interacting with others (such as one's subordinates), attending meetings, and, in general, acting in a management capacity. One British study found evidence of physical stress linked to age and level of responsibility among 1,200 managers sent by their companies for annual medical examinations. The older and more responsible the executive, the greater the probability of the presence of symptoms of heart disease (Pincherle, 1972).

Career development

Interestingly, the third set of environmentally stressful conditions—those relating to career development—appear to have been studied more by physicians than by social psychologists. As a result, there is considerable tendency to relate thwarted career development to psychiatric and psychosomatic symptoms as such and to do so based on individual case experience.

Career-development conditions seen as stressful include overpromotion, underpromotion, status incongruence, lack of job security, and thwarted ambition. In short, stress reactions seem to be a consequence of chronic work frustrations and a disparity between the individual's perception of where he or she should be in a work organization in contrast to the reality.

Alexis Brook (1973) provided a series of interesting case studies of individuals showing behavioral disorders as a result of being either overpromoted with responsibility exceeding capacity or underpromoted with responsibility that is not commensurate with level of competence. In each case, the progression of apparent emotional reaction was from minor psychological symptoms and psychosomatic complaints to more serious mental disorder. Quite a number of authors have linked frustrated work aspirations to mental disorder, and this has led some of them to allege that chronic job stressfulness is a causative factor in psychiatric disability, which merits worker compensation (see Chapter 1).

The fact that career-development issues have received considerable medical scrutiny does not mean that the conclusions drawn from largely anecdotal case reports are either more or less valid than the conclusions of researchers who rely on correlational analysis. Generalizing from a series of cases is common practice in the medical literature, but it does not necessarily lead to statistically sound conclusions or clearly demonstrated causal relationships.

Relationships at work

A number of conditions at work that have been identified as sources of stress concern the relationship with one's superior, subordinate, and peers. Good relationships among members of a work group are a central factor in individual and organizational health. French, Caplan, and Kahn at the University of Michigan relate the mistrust of persons one works with to high role ambiguity, low job satisfaction and feelings of job-related threat to one's well-being. There is also considerable anecdotal evidence from physicians and clinical psychologists supporting the relationship between subordinates and their authority figures with symptoms of emotional disability reported occasionally when that relationship is psychologically unhealthy for one reason or another. Very little empirical work is available, however, concerning *how* this particular stressor condition may contribute to physical and mental illness.

Organizational structure and climate

The fifth potential condition that Cooper and Marshall list among their categories is "being in the organization"; that is, those aspects of the structure of an organization that can make working life either satisfactory and supportive or stressful. Examples of stressful aspects would be little or no participation in decision-making processes that relate to one's job, restrictions on flexibility of work behavior, and interference with desirable communications processes.

The early work on participation was related to its effect on productivity, and much of the seminal work was done by John French and his colleagues at Michigan. For example, Coch and French examined three degrees of participation in a sewing factory. They found that the greater the participation the higher the productivity and job satisfaction and the better the relationships between supervisor and subordinate. French and others subsequently duplicated the experiment in a footwear factory in Norway where greater participation led to significantly more favorable attitudes by workers toward management and more involvement in their job.

French's more recent work found that people who reported greater opportunities for participation in decision making said that they had lower job-related feelings of threat and higher feelings of self-esteem. In another study from Michigan, Margolis and his colleagues (1974) found that nonparticipation in decisions about one's work was the most consistent and significant predictor of "strain and job-related stress." Working with a national representative sample of more than 1,400 workers, they found that nonparticipation was significantly related to: (1) overall poor physical health, (2) escapist drinking, (3) depressed mood, (4) low self-esteem, (5) low job satisfaction, (6) low motivation to work, and (7) intention to leave one's job.

RESPONSIBILITY FOR PEOPLE

To conclude this chapter, let me move away from Cooper and Marshall's excellent classification of conditions associated with perceived job stressfulness to present a few statistics for one job which is said to be unusually stressful—my own.

Physicians who have direct and indirect responsibility for many lives are among the most frequently cited professionals vulnerable to stress reactions. For the most part, they are fortunate in having chosen, and successfully achieved, a role in a highly regarded profession with a great deal of autonomous control over their day-to-day activities. In their case, my case, stressors may be regarded as self-imposed; none of the job constraints of the construction laborer, for example, apply. Economically they are as a group extraordinarily well off.

Yet, in spite of this, one-fourth of the deaths among physicians between the ages of twenty-five and forty-four are suicides. This is compared to 8.5 percent of deaths of white male nonphysicians in that age group. The suicide rate of women physicians is three times higher than that of women in the general population. Physicians have an extraordinarily high rate of alcoholism and drug abuse. Indeed, when I was on the staff of the U.S. Public Health Service Hospital in Lexington, Kentucky, in the 1950s (*the* center for treatment for drug addiction at that time) some 10 percent of our population at all times were physicians. Depending on the statistics you read, the rate of narcotic addiction among physicians is between thirty and one hundred times that of the general population.

Obviously, these factors may be related less with the occupation of physician than with the type of personality that chooses the life of a doctor. They may be much more the consequence of long, irregular working hours, exposure to illness, and various sorts of working conditions. Nevertheless, many feel that the sheer burden of responsibility for other people's safety and health is the key variable.

Physicians are not alone. Many executives see their jobs as similar to the physician's and identify with such statistics. "Dollars, stockholders' dividends, market changes, all those are just numbers," said one vice-president of a large manufacturing company. "They bother me, sure, but the decisions that eat away at me are the ones that involve people. If I have to lay off the father of a family, or deny a transfer to someone, or call someone on the carpet, I'm a wreck for days."

COMMENT

The research into stressful events and stressful conditions is ambiguous at best. But strong and cogent arguments clearly establish that the need to adapt to change at work is stressful, that the increasing pace of technological change calls for the need to adapt which many do not have without breakdown, and that there *are* conditions that are obviously associated with an increased incidence of stress reactions and with higher-than-expected rates of stress-related disease.

But there is other compelling evidence which suggests that occupations or events alone do not determine these stress reactions and these stress-related diseases. Rather, all those antecedents that go to make an individual a laborer or a physician, a shift worker or one on steady daylight hours, form a substrate which is the more important determinant of reaction to life's stressors. Both occupational choice and the meaning of one's work are largely determined by personality factors laid down well before one enters the labor force. It is these characteristics which I believe are far more important in determining possible stress reactions than the simple statistical correlations this chapter describes. Individual vulnerability, then, continues to be the most important of our three variables.

REFERENCES

Breslow, I, and P. Buell (1960). Mortality from coronary heart disease and physical activity at work in California. *The Journal of Chronic Diseases,* **11:** 615-626.

Brook, A. (1973). Mental stress at work. *The Practitioner,* **210:**500-506.

Coch, L., and J. R. P. French (1948). Overcoming resistance to change. *Human Relations* **11:** 512-532.

Cooper, Cary L., and Judi Marshall (1976). Occupational sources of stress: a review of the literature relating to coronary heart disease and mental ill health. *Occupational Psychology,* **49:**11-28.

French, J. R. P., and R. D. Caplan (1970). Psychosocial factors in coronary heart disease. *Industrial Medicine,* **39:**383-397.

French, J. R. P., C. J. Tupper, and E. I. Mueller (1965). Workload of university professors. (Unpublished research report). Ann Arbor: University of Michigan.

Kornhauser, A. (1965). *Mental Health of the Industrial Worker.* New York: Wiley.

Margolis, B. L., W. H. Kroes, and R. P. Quinn (1974). Job stress: an unlisted occupational hazard. *Journal of Occupational Medicine* **16** (10): 654-661.

Pincherle, G. (1972). Fitness for work. *Proceedings of the Royal Society of Medicine* **65** (4):321-324.

Russek, H. I., and B. L. Zohman (1958). Relative significance of heredity, diet and occupational stress in CHD of young adults. *American Journal of Medical Sciences* **235:**266-275.

Schon, D. A. (1972). *Beyond the Stable State.* New York: Random House.

Selye, H. (1974). *Stress Without Distress.* New York: J. B. Lippincott.

Smith, M., M. Colligan, R. W. Horning, and J. Hurrell (1978). Occupational comparison of stress-related disease incidence. Cincinnati: National Institute for Occupational Safety and Health, March.

7

SOCIAL
SUPPORT SYSTEMS

INTRODUCTION

". . . prolonged circumstances which are perceived as dangerous, as lonely, as hopeless, may drain a man of hope and of his health; but he is capable of enduring incredible burdens and taking cruel punishment when he has self-esteem, hope, purpose and a belief in his fellows."

HAROLD G. WOLFF*

Through personal and organizational systems and techniques, stress *can* be managed for most people. The context of work can often be made supportive and individual vulnerability can be reduced. This and the next two chapters start with purely preventive measures, move on to more definitively therapeutic measures, and present a purely personal self-assessment scheme.

Let's first look at some of the organizational supports which can buffer the individual at risk—the employee. In the chapter on context we examined some of the principles which contribute to stress reduction. Here I will be more specific.

---

* Quoted in *Journal of the American Medical Association*, Editorial, **209**: 1082, August 18, 1969.

EMOTIONAL CLIMATE CONTROL

A key word, once again, is "change." A major environmental prop for the individual derives from a climate that allows that person to cope successfully with the inevitable and continuing changes at work. There is today a strong need for the supports which allow the individual to adapt flexibly to change. I emphasize that this emotional climate control must be continuous. There is always a danger that organizations will backslide and follow the old pattern of crisis intervention—contingency management of emergency patchwork at times of dramatic events and transitions. Sound prevention programs may include an occasional "fix," but the major thrust should be ongoing—built into the fabric of the organization.

When the well-established emotional climate of an organization reflects genuine concern for the legitimate needs of its people; when there is esteem and regard for employees—then and only then may individual values blend successfully with the purpose of the organization. The goal of the organizational context in this scheme is to build a system in which people perceive themselves as genuinely valued; where there is adequate communication to enable legitimate individual needs to be met.

A major principle underlying stress management by emotional climate control is the recognition that for the employee who must operate at the same time in many complex contexts (some of which may be in turmoil, others perhaps threatening), no simplistic concept of motivation will do. No manipulative or gimmicky measure will be truly helpful.*

The very basis of a supportive context is the unequivocal involvement of employees in both their own tasks and their occupational destiny. Aside from assuring a healthy respect for the individual, involvement provides both subjective and objective rewards for the organization—rewards which cannot be purchased or easily measured. For more than fifty years, behavioral scientists and a variety of experts concerned with issues of job satisfaction have urged increasing worker participation in defining and programming their tasks.

In the late 1940s, Coch and French demonstrated that the mastery of a new task best takes place under supportive conditions. Looking at

---

* See H. Levinson, *The Great Jackass Falacy*, Division of Research, Harvard Business School, Cambridge, 1973.

the work process in a pajama factory, they found that worker participation in planning the job sharply reduced the time needed to get back to full production after a change in the nature of the task. An invitation from management to participate in the planning and implementation of a change is certainly an environmental support to the self-esteem of workers. One can easily argue that *any* support to self-esteem facilitates individual coping.

Discussion is also useful in coping with the stress of change. Talking with one's peers, superiors, and subordinates allows people to vent whatever feelings of anger, tension, and grief they may be experiencing at the loss of comfortable ways of working. There is reassurance in sharing; in discovering that others have the same apprehension, share the same anxieties. And this leads to understanding and a reduced fear of the unknown.

When stressors strike, people often experience a reduction in their ability to understand—they do not hear information about related events accurately or they distort or deny realities which should be clearly discernible. Therefore the reinforcement of information and instruction and the awareness that practicing new roles takes repetition is important in managing occupational stress.

A valuable technique when refocusing the goal and direction of the organization is to enlist the involvement of all who are facing the stress together in future planning. Where there is promise of future participation, success, and real involvement with work, that goal should be emphasized and reinforced. There is, of course, much that an individual employee or manager can do to help himself or herself. While we cannot lose sight of individual responsibility in this process, the focus in this chapter is on *organizational* support systems. Organizational supports which can help individuals cope with stressors are often extensions of sound management principles.

It is important that the organization be able to answer any employee who asks "What's in it for me?" When stress can be anticipated because of the organization's decision to implement realignments, new processes, and reorganizations, much can be done to alleviate stress reactions by providing the maximum possible information to those involved. Employees should be told the reasons for the actions the organization feels it must take. The more information, the less irrational will be the reactions of individuals in the group. The absence of detailed and specific data is the best possible fuel for anxiety, fantasy, and misunderstanding—and when these run rampant, they draw tremendous energy from productivity and performance.

If a stressful situation stems from a planned change, the active involvement of those concerned can do much to alleviate adverse reactions to the change. Participation in the design of one's future work does much to prevent anxiety and depression. As psychiatrist Ralph Hirshowitz says: "Participatory involvement across, and between, echelon levels of organization mobilizes constructive forces for problem solving; commitment to implementation of decisions increases if employees can become architects of their new roles" (p. 13).

SOCIAL SUPPORT SYSTEMS

Researchers increasingly find support for the idea that the more dangerous effects of occupational stress on health may be sharply reduced by "social support." People are said to have social support if they have a relationship with one or more persons that is characterized by relatively frequent interactions, by strong and positive feelings, and by an ability and a willingness to give and take emotional and/or practical assistance in times of need. While the study of social support as an aid to reducing unhealthy stress reactions is less than a decade old, considerable evidence is building up that it has real value.

How does social support buffer the effect of occupational stressors on health? Usually a supportive social relationship with superiors, colleagues, and subordinates at work will directly reduce levels of perceived job stress. Supportive and helpful coworkers are less likely to create interpersonal pressures. Empathic supervisors are a valuable prop to self-esteem. Generally such support makes people feel more positively about themselves and their work. (There can also be strong social support from persons outside the work setting which may help to moderate occupational stressors in the nonwork context. I will come back to that later.)

The involvement of other people alters our initial perceptions of potentially threatening events. Thus social support can mitigate the effect of *potentially* stressful objective situations such as boring work, heavy workloads, or unemployment, by causing people initially to perceive the situation as less stressful. And, insofar as there is a reduction in the perception of stress, there is also a reduction in the manifestation of those psychological and behavioral responses that may produce disease.

Support from spouses mitigates the impact of job dissatisfaction on health by helping the person to recognize that the job is not all-important in the total context of life and the dissatisfactions associated with it may be compensated for by satisfactions and accomplishments outside of work.

Many studies suggest that social support such as group cohesion, interpersonal trust, and liking for supervisors is associated with reduced levels of stress and better health. For example, Seashore (1954) found that as work-group cohesiveness increased, anxiety regarding work-related matters decreased. And in a study of risk factors in coronary heart disease in administrators, engineers, and scientists, Caplan (1971) found that for those who reported poor relationships with their subordinates, there was a positive relationship between role ambiguity and serum cortisol level (an indicator of physiological arousal related to heart disease as well as to stress reactions). Similarly, a positive relationship exists between perceived workload and serum glucose, blood pressure, and smoking for those having poor relationships with others at work. However, among those having good relationships with others, work stress is *not* related to heart disease risk factors (Wardwell, 1973). In one of the studies of job loss and unemployment reported in Chapter 4, perceived stress resulting from unemployment produced elevated cholesterol levels and increased incidence of illness and depression among men with low social support, while those with higher levels of social support appeared to be protected from these consequences.

Existing evidence strongly suggests that social support can mitigate or modify the effects of stressors in general, and occupational stress in particular, on physical and mental health. House and his colleagues at Duke University looked at the relationship between stressors and symptoms of ill health in groups of workers who had good social support systems and in groups that did not. They found that under maximum levels of social support, symptoms of reported ill health increase only slightly, if at all, as stressors increase. In contrast, when social support is minimal, symptoms of ill health increase dramatically as stressors increase. Put another way, perceived stressors bear little or no relationship to ill health when a person enjoys high levels of social support, but when social support is low, symptoms of ill health are high.

In spite of its importance, however, social support should not be considered a substitute for efforts to reduce the incidence of occupational stress reactions. Rather, it should be viewed as having a *potential* for alleviating occupational stressors which cannot be otherwise reduced.

> *Work organizations have no right to expect supervisors and co-workers, much less spouses, friends, and relatives of workers to buffer employees against stresses which the organization could reasonably reduce or prevent entirely. If the effects of stress are sufficiently deleterious that social support is necessary to alleviate these effects, then we ought to be willing to attempt to reduce that stress as much as possible, utilizing social support primarily to buffer people against stresses we cannot reduce.*
>
> (HOUSE AND WELLS, 1978, p. 24)

Most research on social support measures is in terms of our perceptions that others like and trust us, are concerned about our welfare, and are likely to be of assistance in times of need. Perhaps the critical aspect of effective social support is the establishment of a perception of organizational willingness and ability to help with work-related problems. Social support derived from just one important other individual can be quite effective in mitigating the effects of stress on health; and, in fact, support from additional sources may offer little or no additional benefits.

The work supervisor as that one person is a logical focus for intervention programs. Not only are many supervisors capable of providing effective social support, they can also be influenced through existing organizational channels to perform this duty. In fact, many current programs of supervisory and management training emphasize goals related to social support, and these should certainly be strengthened and more carefully focused. One may conclude that with such techniques, supervisory support is a viable and effective mechanism for mitigating the effects of occupational stressors on health.

DECISION MAKING

There are ways in which organizations can improve the quality of their decision-making processes in the interest of enhancing social support, and these can add immeasurably to the continuing process of stress management. There are several conditions that increase the malfunction which may occur in the decision-making progress and these may interfere with ongoing programs which may be part of stress prevention in a work setting. This list refers entirely to decision making by the chief executive, but it is applicable to other managers in any organization.

1   When the chief executive and his or her staff agree too rapidly on the nature of the problem and on a single response to it.

2   When staff advisers work out their own disagreements over alternative possibilities without the chief's knowledge and then present him or her with a single recommendation.

3   When the staff agrees privately among themselves that the chief should face up to a distressing situation, but no one is willing to tell him or her.

4   When the decision maker is largely dependent upon a single channel of information.

5   When there is no advocate for an unpopular opinion.

6   When the staff takes up alternatives with the chief but covers only a very limited range of options.

7   When the underlying assumptions of a plan have been evaluated only by the advocates of that option.

8   When the chief executive does not arrange for well-qualified consultants to examine carefully the negative judgment offered by one or more staff on a course of action.

9   When the chief is impressed by a consensus among his or her advisers but does not thoroughly examine the adequacy of its basis. (Hamburg and Hamburg, 1980)

Making *explicit* these sources which interfere with effective problem solving and social support systems ultimately enhances future opportunities for dealing with stressful decision-making situations. Both the chief executive and his or her subordinate managers should be able to bring such potential barriers to organizational function more fully into open dialogue. The *process* which leads to decision making needs all the help it can get and all the input those involved can provide. The principles are the same at any organizational level.

MICRO SUPPORT SYSTEMS

On May 11, 1978 the President of the United States met with Mr. George Meany, President of the American Federation of Labor and Congress of Industrial Organizations. President Carter was seeking voluntary restraints on both wages and prices and had expected labor leaders to follow the lead of corporate executives who had previously met with him and pledged to try to use restraint in keeping down prices.

A labor leader who attended the meeting said that "chemistry" was responsible for the result of the meeting which led to an apparent decline in the relationship between the president and Mr. Meany. "They don't speak the same language," he said. "It's like one person speaking in French, and the other speaking in Russian. The president asked Meany if he accepted the principle of deceleration of inflation, and Meany said, 'You're asking me to decelerate wages, and that means a number that is less than last year's.' "

The spokesman said that some of the union leaders present were sympathetic to the president's position. "We wanted to cooperate," he said, "but the climate was such that it was impossible for any of us to speak up after the brouhaha between Meany and the president."

If they had spoken out, he said, the union leaders "would have lynched us" (New York Times).

Obviously, constructive progress toward organizational or national goals cannot be made in an emotional setting of antagonism, anger, or hostility. To be sure, these and similar feelings are relatively common and might be said to permeate much of the emotional climate on and off the job, but they are nonetheless destructive to sound organizational progress. Treatment of these interpersonal skirmishes is not within the scope of this book but acknowledgment of their existence as frequent impediments to progress is important.

One of the reasons for doing so is the influence on the emotional climate of the organization which results from "battles on high." Well-publicized skirmishes at the top management level of any organization encourage polarization down the line and impede constructive action. A coherent leadership philosophy and agreed-upon goals will coalesce warring factions around constructive issues. The working out of episodes of interpersonal friction can lead to the formulation of important organizational goals and to sound micro systems of support for everyone in the organization.

SUMMARY

Support systems for the individual in the organization stem from the fundamental policies, the economic success, and the administrative practices of each work organization. In this chapter we have seen anecdotal examples and research support which suggest there is a great deal the management of an organization can do to provide the work environment most conducive to healthy behavior on the job. From worker involvement in decisions which directly affect his or her labors to the decision-making process to leadership techniques the *organization* can stimulate constructive and productive behavior with a minimum of conflict. In these few pages the psychosocial work environment as supportive of healthy employee adaptation could not be deeply explored. Such exploration, fortunately, is readily available in the Addison-Wesley series of volumes on organizational behavior and in a wide range of writings on occupational mental health and organizational stress and in many of the other books in this series on occupational stress.

REFERENCES

Caplan, R. D. (1971). Organizational stress and individual strain: a social psychological study of risk factors in coronary heart disease among administrators, engineers and scientists. Ph.D. dissertation, University of Michigan.

Coch, L., and J. R. P. French (1948). Overcoming resistance to change. *Human Relations* 11: 512-532.

Hamburg, D. A., and B. A. Hamburg (in press). Occupational stress, endocrine changes, and coping behavior in the middle years of adult life. In L. Levi, *Society, Stress, and Disease & Working Life.* New York: Oxford University Press.

Hirschowitz, R. G. (1973). "Organizational adaptation and the management of transition." Mimeo. Cambridge: Laboratory of Community Psychiatry, Harvard Medical School.

House, James S., and James A. Wells (1978). Occupational stress, social support and health. In Alan McLean (ed.), *Reducing Occupational Stress.* Cincinnati: National Institute for Occupational Safety and Health. (DHEW (NIOSH) Publication No. 78-140.)

New York Times, May 12, 1978.

Seashore, S. (1954). Group cohesiveness in the industrial work group. Ann Arbor: Institute for Social Research, University of Michigan.

Wardwell, W. J. (1973). A study of stress and coronary heart disease in an urban population. *Bulletin of the New York Academy of Medicine* 49 (6): 521-531.

8

PERSONAL STRESS MANAGEMENT

As we have seen stress reactions *can* include psychiatric disability and, in the particularly vulnerable person, *can* trigger major disability. And there is no way that any simple advice can be presented here to change deeply ingrained personality characteristics or coping mechanisms. Words cannot lift a severe depression, or help the reader overcome an acute panic reaction, or bring seriously unrealistic thinking back from the brink of paranoia. There is no way to read this or any other chapter and, as a result, overcome alcoholism or a neurosis.

There *are* however many other ways to improve one's ability to cope with the threat of less serious emotional problems—to reduce to some degree one's vulnerability. Some techniques are purely intellectual, some involve physical and emotional exercises, and some involve more orthodox therapeutic intervention by professionals. And, while it is not within the province of this book to detail all such techniques, help *is* available for those with *any* psychiatric disorder.

I am concerned here with what may be thought of as the garden variety of stress reactions—the most common responses of people who experience and react to serious stressful events, who may be particularly vulnerable or who may not be surrounded by strong support systems. This chapter is for those who are experiencing stress reactions or who wish to develop preventive techniques to cope more effectively with life's day to day stressors.

This chapter builds on the ideas of the first seven chapters. The suggestions may help prevent or help deal with experiences such as those faced by Tom in Chapter 2 whose stomach lining was shown to react so clearly to anger, fear, anxiety, and depression in the daily course of his life experiences. This chapter is for the individual who has been and is now generally able to function productively in life but would like to explore the possibilities of coping with occupational stressors more successfully.

I do not wish to dismiss the problems of people who suffer from incapacitating or prolonged emotional illness. Too many authors of "how to do it" volumes fail to appreciate the limitations of their counsel, and I feel that a disclaimer clearly belongs up front in this discussion of coping techniques. There are times when a readily reversible emotional reaction may at first seem to be a major mental illness. Some quite dramatic symptoms reverse themselves in a very short time and with very little intervention. On the other hand, there are times when the severity of a reaction to a life event does not seem to square with the mildness of the illness which on the surface appears to be the response. And people with lifelong patterns of chronic maladjustment may encounter short-term stress reactions which are superimposed on their long-term personality disorders but then subsequently lift so that the person reverts to his or her customary, but generally unsatisfactory, ways of coping. With chronic or prolonged emotional disability, the best available professional help should be sought.

PLANNING

One of the few things one can be absolutely certain of in today's rapidly changing technology and volatile and chaotic economy is that the future is unpredictable. This has psychological as well as economic ramifications. Unpredictability can be quite stressful for the individual attempting to cope in an organizational context.

It seems that every year or two people find themselves forced to operate under brand-new rules. Circumstances beyond their control—national, international, social, economic, political, and personal—cause events to happen so rapidly and situations to change so unexpectedly that the old reliable and comfortable formulas are no longer applicable. Just as one learns to adjust to one routine or one technology or one set of economic factors, the ground rules change.

Because change is so rapid, work organizations need to develop quick alternatives and viable substitutions in strategies, plans, and operations. This is more crucial to the survival of an enterprise than ever before. Formerly, organizations placed great reliance on improving predictions and planning. Today and in the near future it would seem that the emphasis should be on learning better strategies for reacting and adapting faster and more successfully. Forecasting is simply not accurate enough anymore. Organizations must learn how to plan for alternatives and for successful adaptation. And this involves far more than objective decision making for the organization and far more than projecting a series of personal goals for the individual. It involves developing ways of coping both for an organization and for the individuals in it. It implies that we should use organizational planning strategies in our personal lives.

In this chapter and the next, as we focus on the individual, the process involves developing techniques for coping with less personal overreaction to unexpected change. It involves coping by learning new psychological strategies (difficult as that may be), coping by knowing one's self even better, and coping by developing reasonable personal checks and balances. Very often it involves the need to develop new personal resources.

One of those resources is the clear need to recognize the inevitability of change and the extraordinary difficulty of predicting the direction and speed of change which is likely to have personal impact in the future. Most people have great difficulty considering life other than as it is at the moment. While some may have fantasies of green pastures with economic security at some far distant point, while some aspire to higher levels of skill and power, and while goal-directed activity is fairly common, the achievement of sought-after goals rarely produces peace of mind. Attaining a goal often fails to provide the anticipated fulfillment.

Why? Aside from the unpredictability of the future, it is easier to think in terms of fantasies and unrealistic goals and aspirations. Facing the likely realities of the unknown is difficult at best and for many seems psychologically impossible.

The new planning strategies that are increasingly applied in an organizational setting seem, strangely, to have been used very rarely in _personal_ planning, even by those who apply them best in a business setting. And those who, by mid-career, begin to catch on and take personal corrective action for their own lives tend to concentrate on financial and estate planning rather than consider the need for better ways to adapt to the future and likely stressful events in life.

The personal planning process should be taken up at two levels. At a concrete level, consideration must be given to education, career, geography, monetary needs, family needs, and lifetime goals and objectives. Perhaps more basically one must assess one's strengths and resources as well as one's intellectual and emotional limitations and consider strategies for developing successful coping mechanisms if one is dissatisfied with those one is currently using. Even for those who are comfortable and satisfied with their present coping strategies, periodic reflection is valuable.

The application of planning concepts drawn from the business world is an important aspect of personal stress management. Take the time to periodically reassess goals and aspirations—vocational, social, and personal.

LIFE-CHANGING PHILOSOPHIES

In our world of increasing technical and social change, every aspect of society is being reevaluated and challenged. Traditional values are not so easy to defend. Alternatives seem to appear at a rapid rate. Some are designed to be frankly therapeutic (transactional analysis, behavior modification, reality therapy, logotherapy, psychodrama). Others are geared toward expanded self-awareness and self-actualization (the human potential movement, est, mind control). And there are techniques to reduce high blood pressure, chronic anxiety, and, at the same time, enhance feelings of well-being (biofeedback, the meditation systems, progressive relaxation). Some are concerned with alternative life-styles (Synanon, gay liberation, marriage encounter groups). Many focus on largely physical experience (jogging, massage, Rolfing, bioenergetics, the martial arts). Different sexual experiences become the focus for some (from swinging to sex therapy). Still others involve the rebirth of old and the development of new religious and quasi-religious philosophies and activities (fundamentalism, the Unification Church, the Jesus People, Zen, Om). And there is increased interest in the occult, in altered states of consciousness, and in experimentation with a wide variety of mind-altering drugs.

If I seem to be lumping the "lunatic fringe" with the scientifically respectable, the peripheral neophilosophers with accepted practitioners, I apologize. But the range of new ideas and new systems for self-fulfillment and stress reduction is vast and covers a span from the seemingly idiotic to the rather acceptable to even the relatively conservative clinician.

In particular, our pseudosophisticated Western world seems to be turned on by superficially appealing pseudophilosophies which grant approval to self-indulgence. Not only is it all right, but it becomes mandatory to "look out for Number One." And some of the techniques to reduce anxiety and, apparently, to enhance self-esteem also fly in the face of psychological reality and traditional Western culture. The attainment of Nirvana is not possible for most of us. Anxiety, depression, and mildly distorted perceptions of reality are and will remain a continuing part of our existence. Some pain and some suffering are a part of life.

The next section will briefly describe some of the sounder techniques that offer promise for reducing vulnerability and enhancing one's coping abilities and for managing some, but hardly all, stress reactions.

PHILOSOPHICAL AND INTELLECTUAL EXERCISES

In somewhat the same way that an inspirational talk or challenging sermon may provide the stimulus to look at one's life in a different light, so too may new ideas and perspectives assist with the coping process. But the stimulus of new philosophical concepts and intellectual thoughts is unlikely to alter one's state of vulnerability for long, even though some might argue that great teachers over the years have changed the course of human events. Let me illustrate the philosophical-intellectual kind of stimulus to stress reduction by citing the work of Dr. Ralph G. H. Siu. While Dr. Siu had a distinguished career in the federal government in such positions as Chairman of the Research Council of the Department of Army and as a director of the National Institute of Law Enforcement and Criminal Justice, he is better known to me in his current role as a private consultant in social strategy and decision critique. In viewing job stress Dr. Siu relies heavily on Eastern thought—Taoist and Buddhist—and provides some helpful insights not found in the Western context (Siu, 1971, 1977).

In responding to a request for advice on coping with job stress, Dr. Siu said that *first* he would emphasize that all such advice is to be kept between you as an individual and him as your teacher. He would remind you that you are completely enmeshed by organizations—

your employer, your family, your community, your church—each trying to get the most out of you for its own respective purposes. As long as they do not know your innermost thoughts, they are not able to "bend your complete self to their objectives." Because the moment you reveal those thoughts and motivations the organizations will descend upon you and you will lose a sense of freedom, the neo-Taoist would advise you to "be prudent and be silent."

Dr. Siu's second piece of advice is: Observe the cormorant in the fishing fleet. Recall how cormorants are used for fishing. The technique involves a man in a rowboat with about half a dozen or so cormorants, each with a ring around its neck. As the bird spots a fish, it dives into the water and unerringly comes up with it. Because of the ring, the larger fish are not swallowed but held in the throat. The fisherman picks up the bird and squeezes out the fish through the mouth. The bird then dives for another and the cycle repeats itself.

To come back to the advice from the neo-Taoist to the modern worker: Observe the cormorant. Why is it that of all the animals, the cormorant has been chosen to slave away day and night catching fish for the fisherman? Were the bird not greedy for fish, or not efficient in catching it, or not readily trained, would society have created an industry to exploit the bird?

Greed, talent, and capacity for learning then are the basis of exploitation. The more you are able to moderate and/or to hide them from society, the greater will be your chances of escaping the fate of the cormorant.

The greatest lure is a reputation. There is nothing bad about having a fine reputation. But to the degree that you make reputation a personal necessity, to that degree will you be enslaved. You should consider an incident involving the Zen Buddhist, Bankei. One day while he was giving a sermon, he was continually being interrupted by a Shinsu priest. So Bankei stopped and invited the priest to say what he had on his mind. "The founder of my religion," said the priest, "stood on one bank of a big river, while a disciple stood on the other bank and held a piece of paper. Yet the founder was able to write the holy name of Amida on the paper through the air. Can you perform such a miracle?" "No," replied Bankei, "I can work only little miracles, such as: When I am hungry, I eat. When I am thirsty, I drink. And when I am insulted, I forget."

As to your talents and capacity for learning, never reveal the true extent of your capability except in an emergency. Under ordinary circumstances, take a job that you are capable of doing with only a fraction of your ability. While you are on the job, operate at your cruising level. That is simply sound common sense. Take an automobile rated at 400 horsepower. It is rarely run at that power. The fact of the matter is that it provides a smooth ride only because it is using up but a fraction of its peak power. Similarly, you can be gracious to others only if you yourself are not being strained to the limit. Your pace would be smooth and amenable to telling and gigantic surges when needed because of your large reserve capacity. In this way, you are never apprehensive about doing a highly satisfactory job. Nor are you ever anxious about your ability to handle any emergency that may arise. This frame of mind goes a long way toward serenity.

Dr. Siu's third piece of advice is: Having established your freedom from attachment to work and its rewards and having carved out a chunk of time and energy and psychic reserve you can call your own, you should proceed to harmonize the rest of your doings with nature in accordance with the proper philosophy of life.

If the minimizing of suffering is to be the criterion of good, you should devote your spare time around the office to helping others who are suffering from gross inadequacies, especially those handicapped for one reason or another, even though it may not be your job to do so. Always be available to lend a sympathetic ear to those in trouble. Pay particular attention to individuals as persons rather than to individuals as officials of organizations. The latter are not really persons but more like "impersons."

During after-hours, it might be well to select community affairs in which the beneficiaries would be the poor, the ignorant, and the suffering. There are many other people who will take care of the arts, orchestras, institutions of higher learning, professional societies, and other activities devoted to the maximizing of happiness. It is recognized that the connections you will make for advancement in your professional life by helping the bewildered, the downtrodden, and the unfortunate, will not be as important as those you would make in assisting the affluent, the learned, and the famous. But the minimizing of suffering *per se* will bring the greater meaning of goodness into your living.

Finally, a part of your free time and energy should be given to an avocation of a special kind. This avocation should be one that can be carried out by you alone and that can be employed as a link with nature. Typical examples are composing poetry and painting. This is not to be treated lightly as a hobby to amuse yourself at odd moments but as something serious and enjoyable at the same time. It is to be continued on a regular basis. It is more important that you put in an hour or two every day and six hours or so every weekend, for example, than to put in twenty hours or so at a stretch every weekend or two. If you follow such a routine, retirement will not bring an abrupt change in your pattern of living. You will simply be spending more hours on your avocation, which had been your primary source of satisfaction and pleasure. Work, which you can take or leave as an impersonal relationship on your part with an impersonal organization, is now no longer taking up your time.

In some respects, this way of life resembles that adopted by high officials of imperial China centuries ago. They had free afternoons from the office to devote to amateur archeology, searching for highly prized bronzes, stones, and stela with ancient inscriptions, to painting, to composing poetry, and to calligraphy. Participation in these avocations gave them a feeling of communion with their ancestors, as well as their descendants to come in the universe beyond themselves (Siu, 1971).

This charming interpretation of Eastern thought is, for me, quite seductive. But freedom from attachment to work and its rewards is difficult in our culture. Dr. Siu espouses it as a positive value, but any attempt to modify Western (and more particularly American) cultural norms that link productivity to self-esteem may result in a more stressful situation for the individual than his or her current state of homeostasis no matter how stressful. Suffice it to say that cross-cultural advice is fraught with problems of its own. The point is simply that predetermined cultural reactions may be just as difficult to change as deeply rooted personality characteristics.

Chinese baseball

In addressing himself to the particular problems that management faces and in offering one solution, Dr. Siu does so with a single example.

> This example pertains to the debate not too many years ago regarding the deployment of the antiballistic missile system in this country. When President Nixon took office, he asked Congress for authority to deploy the antiballistic missile system to protect a few American cities against small-scale nuclear attack. When Congressional opposition mounted a fairly strong argument

against the proposal, President Nixon suddenly announced that the purpose of the ABM was not that. That was not practical. His actual purpose was the protection of our own intercontinental ballistic missiles so that they would be able to survive a foreign attack and deliver a counter-blow. Such a shift caught the opposition off guard, and Mr. Nixon obtained approval for the deployment of two ABM sites by a one-vote margin in the Senate.

The following year the President came back to Congress for more funds to deploy additional ABMs. By this time the Congressional opposition had consolidated its own analyses to show that the use of ABM to protect our ICMs was not cost effective. But no sooner did it begin to make points, when Mr. Nixon casually stated in a news conference that the ABMs were not designed to protect our own missiles but to protect all American cities against small-scale nuclear attack. The carefully prepared brief on the part of the anti-ABM cadre was again caught off base at the time and point of action.

With this example of the milieu in which top executives operate before us, can we identify the singularly essential art that characterizes the philosopher-executive? The answer is yes—easily. The singularly essential art is Chinese baseball.

The game of Chinese baseball is played almost exactly like American baseball—the same players, same field, same bats and balls, same method of keeping score, and so on. The batter stands in the batter's box, as usual. The pitcher stands on the pitcher's mound, as usual. He winds up, as usual, and zips the ball down the alley. There is one and only one difference. And that is: After the ball leaves the pitcher's hand and as long as the ball is in the air, anyone can move any of the bases anywhere.

In other words, everything is continually changing—not only the events themselves, but also the very rules governing the judgments of those events and the criteria of value. The secret of Chinese baseball then is not only keeping your eyes on the ball, but also keeping them on the bases—and doing some nimble-footed kicking of the bases yourself.

This kind of situation is alien to the scientific tradition of fixed boundary conditions, clearly defined variables, objective assessments, and rational consistency within a closed system. In the ball game of life, everything is flux and all systems are open.

> *There is no such thing as an occupational stress problem which can be solved for all time and forgotten about, like a mathematical problem of two plus two equals four. There are only occupational stress issues—never fully delineated, never completely resolved, always changing, always in need of alert accommodation.*

(SIU, 1978, p. 136)

To conclude this example of straightforward advice from an Eastern perspective, let me quote ten of Dr. Siu's time-proven, self-explanatory, and specific guidelines for day-to-day activities. As he put it, these proverbs were designed for the "journeyman executive trying to become a philosopher-executive."

Five proverbs for planning are:

1. *The bird hunting the locust is unaware of the hawk hunting him.*
2. *The mouse with but one hole is easily taken.*
3. *In shallow waters, shrimps make fools of dragons.*
4. *Do not try to catch two frogs with one hand.*
5. *Give the bird room to fly.*

Five proverbs for operations are:

1. *Do not insult the crocodile until you have crossed the river.*
2. *It is better to struggle with a sick jackass than carry the wood yourself.*
3. *Do not throw stone at mouse and break precious vase.*
4. *It is not the last blow of the ax that fells the tree.*
5. *The great executive not only brings home the bacon but also the applesauce.*

(SIU, 1978, pp. 143–144)

The wisdom of Ralph Siu's advice is cloaked with a deft touch of humor. But beneath the anecdotes lie philosophical and intellectual thoughts which are both provocative and challenging. In developing a personal approach to stress management, a slightly altered perspective can help to put the reality in balance. A different point of view can often provide the stimulus to rethink one's formulation of a real or potentially stressful situation.

MORE ACTIVE COPING STRATEGIES

There has been a great deal of interest in physical and mental exercises for the essentially healthy person to aid in more successful adapation. I have chosen four examples which are commonly prescribed by various stress-management programs. Subsequent volumes in this series will deal with these and others in more detail. As illustrations which are helpful to some in reducing vulnerability to life's stressors, I have chosen meditation, physical exercise, progressive relaxation, and biofeedback.

Meditation

The term meditation is most often applied to any state of prolonged focus or reflection upon a word, subject, or object. When the concentration is on an object such as a candle flame or a crucifix, the eyes remain open; otherwise, they are more likely to be kept closed. Some forms of meditation require that the individual concentrate on specific body functions such as breathing or heart rate. Meditation is generally performed in the sitting position in a quiet room with subdued lighting. Experienced meditators, however, are able to meditate in noisy rooms, on commuter trains and buses, and in areas which would seem distracting to most people.

In any event, most of the more commonly practiced meditative techniques have been shown to promote relaxation and, at least temporarily, to decrease oxygen consumption, breathing rate, and heart rate, and to alter skin conductance in a manner generally considered indicative of lowered stress. There are also claims (but not much supportive clinical research) that suggest greater resistance to stressors, a reduced amount of psychosomatic illness, and greater emotional stability.

There are many variations of meditation, and I will briefly discuss two and describe one in detail. They are *Trancendental Meditation*, *Benson's Technique*, and *Clinically Standardized Meditation*. They have in common the need to adapt a passive attitude with reduced physical and mental stimuli. Each calls for the repetitive use of a word or a thought (a mantra). Each has a purpose of attaining an altered state of consciousness in which the mind usually is free of extraneous thought.

While the initial object of concentration is thought by most present-day researchers to be in itself rather meaningless and irrelevant to the process of meditation, some recent pilot studies suggest the possibility that different sounds repeated internally may actually have differing effects on mood. However, whatever the ultimate findings on the specificity of the mantra, the main purpose of the meditational object is to serve as a device for clearing the mind of all other thoughts and it tends to facilitate the inducement of some degree of altered consciousness.

It is important to recognize that this is not necessarily a trance-like state, although sometimes it may show characteristics of a very light trance in the same manner that becoming totally absorbed in listening to a concert or in reading an exciting book may bring about a partial shutting out of awareness of the external world. At other times, however, meditation may simply involve an enhanced awareness of one's physical body or emotions; the simple Western forms of meditation do not involve any radical alterations in our orientation to reality. Meditation has at times been described as mystical, however, and others speak of it as a route toward closer contact with the less conscious levels of awareness.

Transcendental meditation

In the late 1950s Marharishi Mahesh Yogi introduced the practice of Transcendental Meditation into the United States. TM has been widely publicized and popularized, with more than a million people having enrolled for instruction at one time or another. Considerable mystique and ritual surround the teaching and practice of TM. The popular literature from the organization does not include instructions on how to perform it and trainees must sign a contract that says they will not reveal certain aspects of the training ritual. The popular press has provided sufficient information to tell us that mantras are assigned and that the meditation environment should have certain specified characteristics.

One of the most advertised benefits for TM is that of increased ability to cope with stress reactions and a reduction in physical measurements associated with such reactions. Yet similar results can be achieved from the relaxation response system of Herbert Benson and the Clinically Standardized Meditation program of Patricia Carrington, each of which is completely open about its processes, programs, and clinical and research results.

Benson's technique

After studying the results of TM, Herbert Benson, a cardiologist at Harvard Medical School, devised a simple form of breathing meditation which he fully described in his book, *The Relaxation Response* (1975). After considerable research, he found that his technique elicited essentially the same physiological changes as TM. (His book is also an excellent general introduction to meditation concepts).

He recommends a passive attitude, a quiet environment, a comfortable position, and a mantra (he recommends the word "one"). With closed eyes, one attempts to relax skeletal muscles and to breathe comfortably. During each expiration one silently repeats the mantra, continuing the process for twenty minutes. The individual is encouraged to use the mantra to block extraneous thoughts from conscious awareness. The process requires considerable concentration and, in this way, differs from the Carrington technique described below. For a few minutes after discontinuing the mantra the individual remains with eyes closed and then gradually opens them to complete the meditation sequence.

Clinically standardized meditation

More recently, Dr. Patricia Carrington has developed Clinically Standardized Meditation (CSM) in response to a need for a somewhat more "permissive" form of meditative relaxation. It was created by modifying a classical form of mantra meditation so that it became a relaxation technique more suitable for Western use. A standardized set of procedures was then adapted, experimented with, and later elaborated upon. The process took several years to complete.

Dr. Carrington has since written the most complete and most readable book on meditation presently available. The following excerpt details her process. I include it here to demonstrate that meditation is not mystical and to illustrate the simplicity of the technique.

Preparation

1. Plan your meditation sessions so you will not be meditating within an hour's time after having eaten a meal, and avoid stimulants such as coffee, tea, or Coca-Cola for one hour beforehand. A small glass of orange juice, milk, or decaffeinated coffee can be taken before meditating. . . . The meditative traditions insist that meditation is relatively ineffective (if not actually harmful) on a full stomach and the reasons for not taking a stimulant are obvious—meditation is for calming down.

2. Choose a relatively quiet room to meditate in where you can be alone, and silence the telephone. Meditation should be under-

taken in a serious manner with few distractions. Explain to others that you are not to be interrupted . . .

3. Meditate seated before a green plant, flowers, or some other natural object where it is pleasant to rest your eyes . . .

4. Face away from any direct source of light. The room need not be dark, but it's pleasanter if the lighting is subdued.

5. Sit on a chair or on the floor, whichever you prefer, in an easy, comfortable position . . . It will help you to relax if you remove your shoes and loosen all tight clothing before commencing to meditate.

6. If during meditation you find yourself uncomfortable at any point you can always change your position slightly, stretch or yawn, or scratch an itch. The point in this type of meditation is to be comfortable. You are not learning the more rigorous forms of meditation such as a Zen monk or a yogi might practice, so you do not have to be concerned with learning to master distractions as they do. This is to be an easy, quiet time with yourself—that is all.

7. . . . If, despite all precautions, you are interrupted during the meditation, remember one thing: to play for time. Try not to jump up out of meditation suddenly any more than you would jump up from a deep sleep if you could avoid it, your body is likely to be as relaxed during meditation as during the deepest stages of sleep. If someone is knocking on the door or calling to you, answer only after a pause (if possible) and say you will be there in a minute or so. Move slowly, yawn, stretch—and then get up. If feasible, return to your meditation after the interruption to finish off the remainder of your meditation time.

8. The best way to time your meditation is by occasionally looking at your clock or watch through half-closed eyes, squinting so as not to alert yourself . . .

9. After finishing meditation, remain seated for a minute or two with your eyes closed. During this time allow your mind to return to everyday thoughts. After a couple of minutes of just sitting, open your eyes very slowly. You may want to rub your hands together gently and run them lightly over your cheeks as though in a face-washing motion, or to stretch. Then rise in a leisurely manner.

Attitude

Whenever thoughts enter your mind (and they will often do so because that too is part of the meditative process) simply treat these thoughts as you might clouds drifting across the sky on a summer's day. You don't try to push the clouds away. You don't hold onto them. You simply watch them come and go. When you realize that your mind is drifting far away and is caught up in thoughts, gently come back to your object of focus. No forcing— you do this pleasantly, the way you would come home again to greet a good friend. The extraneous thoughts which you had are a natural and useful part of the meditative process.

Keep in mind that you are not to try to make anything "happen" during meditation. Trust the meditation to "know" best. Some people have compared these forms of meditation to the experience of being in a rowboat without oars, gently drifting on a quiet stream. Let the stream take you where it will.

Mantra Meditation

Select one of the three mantras suggested in the list below, or, if you wish, substitute a word of your own choosing which has a pleasant ringing sound. If you decide to create your own mantra, be sure to avoid using any word which is emotionally "loaded." No names of people, no words that bring too intense or exciting an image. The word should ring through your mind and give you a feeling of serenity. If it has a touch of unfamiliarity or mystery to it, this can help remove you from everyday thoughts and concerns.

MANTRAS
Ah-nam
Shi-rim
Ra-mah

Having selected your mantra, sit down comfortably. With eyes open and resting upon some pleasant object such as a plant, say the mantra out loud to yourself, repeating it slowly and rhythmically. Enjoy saying your mantra. Experiment with the sound. Play with it. Let it rock you gently with its rhythm. As you repeat it, say it softer and softer, until finally you let it become almost a whisper.

Now stop saying the mantra out loud, close your eyes, and

simply listen to the mantra in your mind. Think it, but do not say it. Let your facial muscles relax, do not pronounce the word, just quietly "hear" the mantra, as, for example "Ah-nam" . . . "Ah-nam" . . . "Ah-nam" . . . That is all there is to meditating—just sitting peacefully, hearing the mantra in your mind, allowing it to change any way it wants—to get louder or softer—to disappear or return—to stretch out or speed up. . . . Meditation is like drifting on a stream in a boat without oars—because you need no oars—you are not going anywhere.

Continue meditating for twenty minutes. When the time is up sit quietly without meditating for a least two or three minutes more (or longer if you wish) then follow the instructions in Point 9 for coming out of meditation. *

While these instructions are sufficient to allow one to begin meditating, let me urge you to obtain personal instruction. Knowledge of potential pitfalls as well as possible individual modifications of the process is necessary if you wish to learn CSM successfully.†

Exercise

The adage that good physical conditioning promotes feelings of emotional well-being seems fairly well established. Moderation in diet and drinking, avoiding cigarettes, and getting appropriate exercise and rest are important to overall good health. These commonplace suggestions do play a role in reducing vulnerability to stressors and, probably, in moderating stress reactions when they do occur. For example, heavy alcohol consumption leading to a hangover produces feelings of irritability, dullness, and a variety of physical symptoms which, when present, increase one's vulnerability to the point that a relatively minor stressor produces an exaggerated stress reaction. Continuous excessive drinking creates all manner of physical and emotional disability, with tissue destruction and metabolic imbalance and is clearly self-destructive behavior.

---

*From Patricia Carrington, *Freedom in Meditation* (Garden City, New York: Anchor Press/Doubleday, 1978), pp. 78–78. Reprinted with permission.

†Readers who wish to learn Clinically Standardized Meditation may obtain a course in CSM taught on tape by Dr. Patricia Carrington, using the same method she uses when giving personal instruction in this technique. The course consists of three one-hour cassettes and a manual. For details on the *self-regulated* CSM *course,* write to Pace Educational Systems Inc., P.O. Box 113, Kendall Park, New Jersey 08824.

The role of a well-balanced exercise program as a prop to general good health as well as stress management is not as well proven as the destructive effects of heavy drinking. Arguments abound on both sides of the issue. Few would argue against a continuing program of exercise as a sound health practice; but many vigorously oppose jogging and heavy exercise for those whose life-style has been sedentary. Indeed, starting an active exercise program at mid-life without careful medical supervision is extremely dangerous. As usual, the proper action lies between the two extremes. Exercise must be tailored to individual health status and personality characteristics. For some, the rocking chair or hammock will do more good on weekends than enforced exertion that is unwelcome. For others, a properly supervised, continuing program of running, swimming, cycling, and walking may be extraordinarily helpful.

Exercises designed to increase the tone of or relax certain groups of muscles are often prescribed for the treatment and control of a great many specific physical problems—and some with psychosomatic components. To the extent that they lead to the reduction of physical discomfort and often a disabling pain, we may assume that they have a role in reducing an individual's vulnerability to stressors.

Two examples from recent studies will illustrate the point. Recently the YMCA invited individuals suffering from back pain to participate in an exercise program. The individuals were self-selected; that is, not referred by physicians. Of the 421 individuals who took part in a six-week program, 65.5 percent had either excellent or good results, 25 percent noted some improvement, and 9 percent had poor results. Whether continuation of such an exercise program will lead to continued control of back pain for this group is speculative. We do know—and it is puzzling—that an extremely large number of people who commence such programs give them up at a later date regardless of how much better they felt during the period of exercise activity.

More germane to this book is the study by Dr. John Greist, an associate professor of psychiatry at the University of Wisconsin who has used running as an antidepressant.

'Tis better to hunt in fields for
health unbought,
Than fee the doctor for a nauseous
draught.
The wise for cure on exercise
depend.   JOHN DRYDEN, circa 1675

Pointing out that up to 10 percent of the population will score in the depressed range on standard depression questionnaires at any one time, Greist and his colleagues invited "normal" college faculty members to participate in six weeks of physical activity. Eleven of the sixty-seven who agreed to participate scored in the depressed range on such a questionnaire measurement of depression. At the completion of the study, each of the eleven "depressed" men had increased his physical fitness and no longer had "depressed" questionnaire scores and none of the other fifty-six individuals scored in the depressed range.

Of 167 college students who exercised three times weekly for eight weeks doing wrestling, tennis, "varied exercises," jogging, or softball, the joggers showed the greatest reduction in depression scores and the softball players and the six students who did not exercise showed no change in the depression score.

Greist and his colleagues then decided to conduct a pilot study to see whether running might have anything to offer to individuals who were indeed moderately depressed in the opinion of psychiatric clinic physicians. Thirteen men and fifteen women patients were randomly assigned to either running or to one of two kinds of individual psychotherapy. The patients were between eighteen and thirty years old, complained of depression as their major symptom, found their depression interfered with important activities, and had high scores on depression checklists.

Those patients assigned to running and who stayed with it for ten weeks did remarkably well. Six of the eight patients who ran had recovered from their depression, a result comparable to the best outcomes obtained by psychotherapy for patients at the clinic and better than those who were assigned to psychotherapy (Greist et al., 1978).

While such a small sample and such a short period of time does not allow us to conclude that running, even under the carefully supervised program devised at the University of Wisconsin, is generally curative of depression, it is suggestive. And certainly one of the most common stress reactions is one form or another of depression. I think we *can* conclude that moderate exercise, tailored to the individual's physical health, together with other habits and behaviors supportive of sound physical health, is a useful personal support system in any individual program of stress management.

Progressive relaxation

In 1929, a physiologist-physician in Chicago, Dr. Edmund Jacobson, recognizing that anxiety was related to skeletal-muscle contraction, developed the idea that the relaxation of these same muscles would logically reduce anxiety level (Jacobson, 1929). He noted that even when the major voluntary muscles were relatively relaxed, there remained a level of muscle tension which, with prolonged and highly specialized exercises, could be further reduced with accompanying feelings of well-being. He therefore put forth the concept of progressively relaxing muscles on a regular basis as a technique to prevent as well as to treat anxiety. In short, Jacobson's technique has as its goal increased control over skeletal muscles until the individual is able to induce very low levels of tension in major muscle groups such as the arms and the legs.

In the forty-five years since he introduced progressive relaxation, Dr. Jacobson has continued to refine the process incorporating instrumentation not unlike that used in biofeedback, refined his techniques of teaching patients, and applied the technique to a wider range of conditions. Among psychiatrists and psychologists, progressive relaxation has met with a mixed reception; it is only rarely prescribed. It has found a certain currency in the popular press and, for some, is a useful technique (Jacobson, 1970).

In a nutshell, progressive relaxation is practiced in a reclining position in a quiet room. A passive attitude is essential since distractions often induce slight but measurable muscle tension. Part of the technique is that the patient is taught to recognize even these minimal muscle contractions particularly around the eyes and face so that he or she can avoid them to achieve the deepest degree of relaxation possible. Seven sets of exercises are proposed relating to the arm, the leg, the trunk, the neck, the eye region, vision, and speech. At least thirty hours are required learning to tense and relax muscles associated with these parts of the anatomy.

While I inferred a lack of great support for the application of progressive relaxation among professionals, I would point out that some evidence is accumulating that progressive relaxation is helpful in a variety of conditions such as sleep disturbance (Borkovek, 1976).

Biofeedback

Just as successful meditation can alter blood flow and blood pressure along with other involuntary bodily functions, so too the process of *biofeedback* can produce even more dramatic results. Professor Neil Miller at Rockefeller University is generally credited with the basic animal research and subsequent human research which has now led to a burgeoning therapeutic application widely used in the control of such illnesses as migraine headache and high blood pressure as a relaxation technique (Miller, 1969). Feedback is a relatively simple process of monitoring one or more physiological functions with measuring devices which translate the recorded activity into audible or visual signals which can be readily perceived by the patient or research subject. The theory is that the individual may, by observing these signals, somehow learn to exercise a degree of control over the particular function being monitored. The individual makes use of this continuous flow of sensory feedback signals to modify his or her ongoing performance in one or another area of function. Through such a process people have been able in a relatively short time to alter the temperature in specific parts of the body such as hands, feet, and forehead and affect certain brain waves as well as their pulse and blood pressure.

One early example cited by Dr. Benson had to do with demonstrating the use of biofeedback in the control of blood pressure. "In this investigation we attached the patients to monitors that kept them informed of momentary rises or falls of blood pressure. Through the use of such feedback, our patients apparently learned to lower their systolic blood pressure level. But when we asked these subjects how they lowered their blood pressures, they said simply they did so by thinking relaxing thoughts" (p. 57).

An entire instrumentation market has developed around the concept of biofeedback with several manufacturers producing devices to monitor and display ongoing physical and mental processes. Some of the applications are quite interesting and deserve brief mention. Some individuals, for instance, who suffer from migraine headaches have had success in reducing or eliminating the pain by using the so-called feedback thermometer. The technique requires that thermocouples be attached to fingers or other parts of the body. The patient then attempts to increase or decrease the temperature in his or her hand. What happens is that, through some poorly understood process, one is able either to increase or to decrease blood flow to extremities. And when there is increased blood flow and increased temperature as a result to the hands, blood pressure in the head tends to decrease and pain subsides.

The electromyograph is a device to measure muscle tension. Muscle relaxation, as we know, is extraordinarily important in a variety of psychosomatic pain. The relief of tension—back pain and head pain—can be achieved through muscle relaxation.

An electromyograph monitor attached to the forehead muscles can provide a patient with feedback on the state of muscle tension in the forehead. As the muscles become more relaxed, the tension head-ache tends to disappear. The same muscle-tension-measurement tech-nique can be used in other muscle groups equally well.

Finally, as an example of biofeedback (and there are a great many more in the literature), there is a device called a dermograph which monitors the electrical conductance of the skin which is sometimes called the galvanic skin response. The conductivity of electricity across a specific section of skin is generally related to the moisture in the skin and the content in that sweat of various minerals which also increase the rate of flow of small quantities of electricity. Many stimuli or stressors may arouse responses in the galvanic skin response which are not consciously apparent to the patient. The dermograph detects this phenomenon, producing a perceptible signal as a result. In effect, the dermograph produces information, not primarily about the particular tissue being monitored, but about the general activity level of the central nervous system. In this instance, the skin is simply a conduit of the flow of information. In this matter, one can detect variations in the intensity of the emotional responses to a stimulus and learn how to control them and thus to control stress reactions.

PROFESSIONAL INTERVENTION

It is important to place in perspective the forms of self-help that I have discussed thus far. Many people *do* reduce their personal vulnerability to stressors by a different outlook on their problems, by meditation, exercise, biofeedback and relaxation techniques, but these and similar methods offer no assurance nor insurance of inoculation against stress reactions. Other techniques such as opening up new avocational inter-ests and exploring new social contacts can also be extremely helpful to some. But for a few, such moves are very difficult and may mobilize more anxiety than they allay.

Chapter 9 suggests some of the professional resources which the person who finds himself or herself without adequate personal re-sources to cope successfully may find useful. But they also deserve mention in our consideration of coping techniques.

Most of the internal and largely unconscious processes that mediate the relationship between stressful events, our context, and our vulnerability and that determine whether or not we will develop a stress reaction take place in a mature adult personality. Much of the way that personality will react is, in effect, predetermined. We have all learned a whole host of coping techniques, defense mechanisms, and reasonably satisfactory ways of getting along—all outside our levels of conscious awareness. We started learning them shortly after birth and have developed quite firmly entrenched styles of dealing with both the outside and our own internal world. These are difficult to change. Perhaps this is why many of the approaches suggested earlier work for a while (often while they are still effective) and then are abandoned; why people get support from fitness programs or meditation or relaxation techniques and then abandon them to revert ways of coping that were learned earlier and that are deeply ingrained.

The most thoroughgoing professional approach to relearning the coping techniques which are an integral and intimate part of our personalities is that of psychoanalysis. It requires literally years of intensive effort with an extraordinarily highly trained professional (usually a physician with psychiatric training and subsequent lengthy work in a psychoanalytic institute). While no one knows the optimum procedure (and it will vary from person to person), at least two to four sessions a week for three to five years can indeed overcome unhealthy ways of coping in some suitable persons (and not all are suitable) and constructively alter unconscious processes which inhibit optimum adaptation. This is the Rolls Royce of professional therapeutic intervention.

If one's goal is not so high, shorter term, psychoanalytically oriented psychotherapy can be most helpful. If one's emotional problem is reasonably well circumscribed, a variety of professional intervention techniques can also be very helpful indeed. Here I am thinking of short-term supportive psychotherapy to clarify issues and help straighten out feelings at a time when one is faced with a turbulent life situation.

Throughout this very brief discussion of professional therapeutic resources, I continue to focus on what most of us think of as the psychopathology of everyday life. I speak of intervention techniques for the relatively healthy. I speak to those who have not lost emotional control, who are very much in touch with reality but whose life-style and whose present circumstances would benefit by deeper insight.

(Other volumes in this series address more specific therapeutic intervention for those with more serious disability; those who are mentally ill in the truer sense of that phrase.)

REFERENCES

Benson, H. (1975). *The Relaxation Response.* New York: Morrow, p. 57.

Borkovek, T. D. (1976). Effects of progressive relaxation on sleep disturbance: An electroencephalographic evaluation. *Psychosomatic Medicine* May-June.

Carrington, P. (1978). *Freedom in Meditation.* Garden City, New York: Anchor Press/Doubleday.

Greist, H. H., M. H. Klein, R. R. Eischens, and J. W. Faris (1978). Antidepressant running. *Behavioral Medicine* 5 (6): 19–24.

Jacobson, E. (1929). *Progressive Relaxation.* Chicago: University of Chicago Press.

_____. (1970). *Modern Treatment of Tense Patients.* Springfield, Illinois: Charles C. Thomas.

Miller, N. E. (1969). Learning of visceral and glandular responses. *Science* 163:434–445.

Siu, R. G. H. (1971). Work and serenity. *Occupational Mental Health* 1:1, pp. 5–6.

_____. (1978). The Tao of organization management. Chapter 14 in Alan McLean (ed.), *Reducing Occupational Stress.* National Institute for Occupational Safety and Health, April. (DHEW (NIOSH) Publication No. 78–140.

9

A METHOD OF
SELF-ASSESSMENT

The first chapters have formed a background for understanding occupational stress, stressors, and stress reactions. In the next few pages I will attempt to make some of these ideas personally useful. As the earlier material developed, it became clear that social support systems are tremendously valuable in forestalling and coping with specific stressors.

One's vulnerability can be reduced by a clear understanding of one's own strengths and weaknesses and an awareness that one's susceptibility to stressors is heightened when we are forced to cope with more than one seriously troublesome event at a time. Even with a supportive environment and reasonably high personal resistance, however, an overwhelmingly powerful stressor is still able to produce symptoms.

This chapter presents the framework for personal assessment of how one deals with job-related stress. One may complete his or her own personal Coping Checklist to compare with an idealized model of one who copes successfully. This is helpful in allowing one to assess where one stands and suggest actions which may be useful to take.

Next there is an exercise which may help one to assess one's own job context; after that, a checklist of stressors. What might be causing problems for you on the job? There is a Stressors Checklist to help you find it out.

Finally there is an opportunity to apply the model of the overlapping circles with an exercise showing the complicated interaction of stressors with one's own individual vulnerability and work environment to illustrate how all these factors, coming together, can produce symptoms of physical or emotional discomfort.

Toward the end of the chapter there is a review of the kinds of assistance available to people who feel they may need some help in coping with the stresses of everyday life on the job—resources to call on if you so desire.

It is important to keep in mind that this brief paper-and-pencil system of checklists and surveys is a very rough approximation of that which it purports to measure. The system hardly produces the results that a detailed, well-validated psychological test in the hands of a competent professional or psychiatric interview would yield. I have purposely called them "worksheets" and "checklists" and used the words "indicators" and "surveys." That's all they are.

In a very gross way, they may reflect general tendencies and suggest the desirability of a more detailed, professional assessment. Keep in mind that "scores" that suggest both healthy adaptation and successful behavior may be as misleading as those that infer an area of concern.

Before moving on to these summary exercises and concluding comments, a warm-up quiz will establish the mood.

ARE YOU A WORKAHOLIC?

A great deal of attention has recently been focused on the problems of the "workaholic." This is an individual whose work has become the dominant factor in life, to the extent that it tends to interfere with the sort of balanced adaptation that most people would regard as "normal."

Consider the following series of questions. They form a reasonable checklist for those who may be concerned that their work is becoming all-encompassing; for those who are a bit fearful that it may be time to take stock and redress balances. If you follow the instructions, you'll discover whether, from my perspective, it is important that you reevaluate the dominance of work in your life or whether it's okay to continue along without concern.

When psychiatrists or psychologists interview patients for symptoms of compulsive work habits, they frequently ask such questions as those presented here. Well adjusted people may give the same answers as those who are obsessed with work, but the true "workaholic" will probably answer nearly all of them as indicated at the bottom of this page. (Actually, professionals rarely interrogate their patients so directly and, unfortunately, few tend to focus on work in understanding an individual's adjustment.)

1   Do you seem to communicate better with your secretary (co-workers) than with your spouse (or best friend)?

2   Are you always punctual for appointments?

3   Are you better able to relax on Saturdays than on Sunday afternoons?

4   Are you more comfortable when you are productive than idle?

5   Do you carefully organize your hobbies?

6   Are you usually much annoyed when your spouse (or friend) keeps you waiting?

7   When you play golf is it mainly with business associates? (or: are most recreational activities with work associates?)

8   Does your spouse (or friend) think of you as an easygoing person?

9   If you play tennis do you occasionally see (or want to see) your boss's face on the ball before a smash?

10   Do you tend to substitute your work for interpersonal contacts; that is, is work sometimes a way of avoiding close relationships?

11   Even under pressure, do you usually take the extra time to make sure you have *all* the facts before making a decision?

12   Do you usually plan every step of the itinerary of a trip in advance and tend to become uncomfortable if plans go awry?

13   Do you enjoy small talk at a reception or cocktail party?

14   Are most of your friends in the same line of work?

15   Do you take work to bed with you when you are home sick?

16   Is most of your reading work related?

17   Do you work late more frequently than your peers?

18   Do you talk "shop" over cocktails on social occasions?

19   Do you wake up in the night worrying about business problems?

20   Do your dreams tend to center on work related conflicts?

21   Do you play as hard as you work?

---

(1) Yes (2) Yes (3) Yes (4) Yes (5) Yes (6) Yes (7) Yes (8) No (9) Yes (10) Yes (11) Yes (12) Yes (13) No (14) Yes (15) Yes (16) Yes (17) Yes (18) Yes (19) Yes (20) Yes (21) Yes (22) Yes (23) Yes

22 Do you tend to become restless on vacation?

23 If you are a homemaker, do you tend to prepare most of the food for the week on Sunday?

THE COPING CHECKLIST

The Coping Checklist is designed to provide a very rough and superficial approximation of how well you are now coping with your job in comparison with the idealized model that I will discuss shortly.

COPING CHECKLIST*

To what extent does each of the following fit as a description of you? (Circle one number in each line across:)

	Very true	Quite true	Some-what true	Not very true	Not at all true
1 I "roll with the punches" when problems come up.	1	2	3	4	5
2 I spend almost all of my time thinking about my work.	5	4	3	2	1
3 I treat other people as individuals and care about their feelings and opinions.	1	2	3	4	5
4 I recognize and accept my own limitations and assets.	1	2	3	4	5
5 There are quite a few people I could describe as "good friends."	1	2	3	4	5
6 I enjoy using my skills and abilities both on and off the job.	1	2	3	4	5
7 I get bored easily.	5	4	3	2	1
8 I enjoy meeting and talking with people who have different ways of thinking about the world.	1	2	3	4	5
9 Often in my job I "bite off more than I can chew."	5	4	3	2	1
10 I'm usually very active on weekends with projects or recreation.	1	2	3	4	5
11 I prefer working with people who are very much like myself.	5	4	3	2	1

*From Alan A. McLean, *Dealing With Job Stress* (cassettes and workbook), copyright 1976, Management Decision Systems, Inc. Reproduced with permission.

	Very true	Quite true	Some-what true	Not very true	Not at all true
12 I work primarily because I have to survive, and not necessarily because I enjoy what I do.	5	4	3	2	1
13 I believe I have a realistic picture of my personal strengths and weaknesses.	1	2	3	4	5
14 Often I get into arguments with people who don't think my way.	5	4	3	2	1
15 Often I have trouble getting much done on my job.	5	4	3	2	1
16 I'm interested in a lot of different topics.	1	2	3	4	5
17 I get upset when things don't go my way.	5	4	3	2	1
18 Often I'm not sure how I stand on a controversial topic.	5	4	3	2	1
19 I'm usually able to find a way around anything which blocks me from an important goal.	1	2	3	4	5
20 I often disagree with my boss or others at work.	5	4	3	2	1

Scoring Directions

Add together the numbers you circled for the four questions contained in each of the five coping scales.

Coping scale	Add together your responses to these questions	Your score (write in)
Knows self	4, 9, 13, 18	_____
Many interests	2, 5, 7, 16	_____
Variety of reactions	1, 11, 17, 19	_____
Accepts other's values	3, 8, 14, 20	_____
Active and productive	6, 10, 12, 15	_____

Then, add the five scores together for your overall total score: _____

Scores on each of the five areas can vary between 5 and 20. Scores of 12 or above perhaps suggest that it might be useful to direct more attention to the area.

The overall total score can range between 20 and 100. Scores of 60 or more may suggest some general difficulty in coping on the dimensions covered.

This checklist is a little more serious than the usual game of twenty questions. Note that your response to each question will range from 1 to 5 (from "very true" to "not at all true"). You will find the instructions for scoring below the questions. After you have completed responding to the twenty items and completed tallying your score, you will arrive at a single numerical coefficient for coping. If it is very high, then you may have some areas of concern; if it is low, you can be fairly well assured that your response to your job situation—the way you are coping with it—is really quite good.

Please keep in mind that nobody measures up ideally; nobody is going to get a score of twenty.

HEALTHY COPING AT WORK

Now look at what would be considered by many to be a model of an ideally successful person and relate it to the Coping Checklist. It has five parts and is really a definition of successful adaptation. *First*, the truly successful and healthy person is one who really knows himself or herself at all levels and who understands and accepts his or her own strengths and own weaknesses. This doesn't mean that such a person lies back acceptingly and says, "Okay, I'm weak in this area; so what!" But he or she knows himself or herself well enough to know those personality factors that can't be changed and those skills—social and professional—on which to capitalize.

Second, such a person is one who, despite stereotypes to the contrary, has developed *a lot* of interests outside the world of work. He or she has a variety of satisfactions in life and does not get all his or her satisfaction from the job. This person has irons in many fires and these interests (as well as those relating to family and business) are regularly pursued.

Third, such a person is one who doesn't always react in the same way to factors that he or she finds stressful. The person who copes successfully doesn't always develop a headache when angry with the boss or always get depressed when faced with an apparently minor threat. Such a person doesn't always become either hyperactive or frozen by incapacity under stressful circumstances. And he or she can bounce back fairly quickly from stress reactions.

Fourth, such a person acknowledges that others have different value systems, different ways of doing things, and tends to accept this as a fact of life without attempting to build others over in either his or her own image.

Fifth, he or she is active and productive at work, without sacrificing similar activity in the community and in the home.

To summarize, a five-point highly idealized model of the successful person coping very well is a person who knows himself or herself, who does not always react the same way, who recognizes that others have different value systems and who doesn't try to change them, and finally, who is active and productive.

This definition gives us a goal. Of course, no one measures up fully in all five areas or even in most of them. But it is a model, and just as we use models in developing other behavior, so too we can use models such as this in trying to establish new coping techniques or to modify some of the ways we now cope.

Next consider a job's context, the environment in which job satisfaction may or may not take place. Following the instructions, go over the items in the Context Survey rating them from 1 to 5 and assess various aspects of satisfaction with your present job.

CONTEXT SURVEY

How do you feel about each of the following on your job? (Circle one number in each line across:)

	Very satis-fied	Satis-fied	Neutral	Dissat-isfied	Very dissat-isfied
1 How satisfied are you with the company you work for compared with other companies you know about?	1	2	3	4	5
2 How satisfied are you with your job—the kind of work you do?	1	2	3	4	5
3 How satisfied are you with your physical working conditions (heat, light, noise, etc.)?	1	2	3	4	5
4 How satisfied are you with the extent to which people you work with cooperate well with one another?	1	2	3	4	5
5 How satisfied are you with the job your immediate supervisor is doing in managing his or her people responsibilities?	1	2	3	4	5

	Very satis- fied	Satis- fied	Neutral	Dissat- isfied	Very dissat- isfied
6 How satisfied are you with the job your immediate supervisor is doing in managing his or her task or functional responsibilities?	1	2	3	4	5
7 How satisfied are you with your pay, considering your duties and responsibilities?	1	2	3	4	5
8 How satisfied are you with your pay, considering what other companies pay for similar types of work?	1	2	3	4	5
9 How satisfied are you with your advancement to better jobs since you started to work with your company?	1	2	3	4	5
10 How satisfied are you with your opportunities to move into a better job in your company?	1	2	3	4	5
11 How satisfied are you with the extent to which your present job makes full use of your skills and abilities?	1	2	3	4	5
12 How satisfied are you with the level of mental ability requirements of your present job (problem solving, judgment, technical knowledge, etc.)?	1	2	3	4	5
13 How satisfied are you with the level of average time demands of your present job (hours worked, as opposed to mental ability demands)?	1	2	3	4	5
14 Now, considering everything, how would you rate your overall feelings about your employment situation at the present time?	1	2	3	4	5

15 If you have your way, will you be working for your present organization five years from now?
Circle one:

1 Certainly   4 Probably not
2 Probably   5 Certainly not
3 I'm not at all sure   0 I'll be retired in five fears

Scoring Directions

Add together the numbers you circled on the Context Survey and enter the total here: _____

Scores on the survey can range between 14 and 75. Scores of 45 or more may suggest that the overall context of your work is less than satisfactory. You should also evaluate the specific items in the survey which you rated negatively.

Next consider the a Stressors Checklist. What's getting to you at work?

STRESSORS CHECKLIST

Listed below are various kinds of problems that may—or may not—arise in your work. Indicate to what extent you find each of them to be a problem, concern, or obstacle in carrying out your job duties and responsibilities. (This checklist obviously does not include possible off-the-job sources of stress.)

This factor is a problem . . .	Never	Sel-dom	Some-times	Usually	Always
Conflict and uncertainty:					
1 Not knowing just what the people you work with expect of you.	1	2	3	4	5
2 Feeling that you have to do things on the job that are against your better judgment.	1	2	3	4	5
3 Thinking that you will not be able to satisfy the conflicting demands of various people over you.	1	2	3	4	5
Job pressure:					
4 Feeling that you have too heavy a workload; one that you can't possibly finish during an ordinary day.	1	2	3	4	5
5 Not having enough time to do the work properly.	1	2	3	4	5
6 Having the requirements of the job impact your personal life.	1	2	3	4	5
Job scope:					
7 Being unclear on just what the scope and responsibilities of your job are.	1	2	3	4	5
8 Feeling that you have too little authority to carry out the responsibilities assigned to you.	1	2	3	4	5

	Never	Sel-dom	Some-times	Usually	Always
9 Not being able to get the information you need to carry out your job.	1	2	3	4	5
Rapport with management:					
10 Not knowing what your manager or supervisor thinks of you—how he or she evaluates your performance.	1	2	3	4	5
11 Not being able to predict the reactions of people above you.	1	2	3	4	5
12 Having ideas considerably different from those of your managers.	1	2	3	4	5

Scoring Directions

Add the three numbers you circled within each of the four areas and enter them here:

Conflict and uncertainty . . . .   _____
Job pressure . . . .   _____
Job scope . . . .   _____
Rapport with management . . . .   _____
Then add the four scores together for your overall total score   _____

Scores on each of the four areas can range between 3 and 15. Scores of 9 or above perhaps suggest that the area may be presenting a problem for you warranting attention.

The overall total score can range between 12 and 60. Scores of 36 or more may suggest a more than desirable amount of overall stress in your job environment.

Next let us look at the interrelationships between the environment or context, individual vulnerability, and stressors and see if it is possible to relate them to *symptoms* in a psychiatric sense. Actually, a job's psychosocial stressors tend to be defined in terms of producing symptoms when context and vulnerability are ripe. That is, one must be in a particularly vulnerable situation, or one's vulnerability must be particularly high, or one must be in an overwhelmingly threatening environment or context if specific stressors are to produce symptoms. For this reason, it is difficult to categorize or to present any kind of listing of stressors since their activity is always in terms of the individual's everchanging vulnerability and context.

The concepts of context, vulnerability, and stressors were introduced as overlapping circles in Chapter 3. The following exercise is built around the use of the three circles.

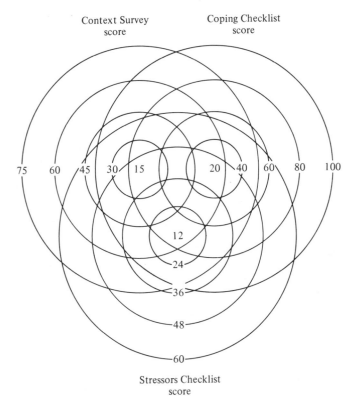

Context Survey
score

Coping Checklist
score

Stressors Checklist
score

FIG. 9.1 *Dealing with job-related stress. For each of the three checklists—the Context Survey, the Coping Checklist, and the Stressors Checklist—find the spot on the scale within the appropriate circle which corresponds to your overall total score. Draw the total circumference of the circle corresponding to that score. After doing this for each of the three scales, the extent to which the three circles overlap may suggest to some degree the extent to which there is stress associated with your current job environment.*

COMPLETING YOUR OWN DIAGRAM

The figure for this exercise shows three overlapping circles, each circle separately numbered. The idea is that on each of the three checklists you locate your numerical score for the appropriate checklist and pencil in the entire circle that corresponds to your score. After doing this for each of the three scales, the extent to which all three may overlap suggests the extent to which there may be stress associated with your current total job environment, including your reactions to it. It may give you greater understanding of your present work situation.

In earlier chapters, I suggested that *if* one can reduce the effect of a specific stressor, or *if* one's vulnerability can be reduced, or *if* factors which make up the environment or the context can be improved, then there would not be any symptoms of response to stressors. The circles of our diagram would not touch, let alone overlap.

One can focus separately on each of the three variables. One can manipulate or reduce or foresee and thus react less strongly to stressors. One can make major efforts to reduce one's vulnerability through some of the techniques described in the last chapter. One can also build a system that is supportive and that contributes to a more supportive context. Each of these techniques minimizes the likelihood of overlapping circles and symptomatic responses.

Should one come to the point of having symptoms, however, one may moderate their influence through the use of counseling and psychotherapy or through direct intervention under medical supervision with medication. There are also a variety of other therapeutic methods which, under professional supervision, are generally effective.

The main point here is that there are several ways of obtaining help in coping with stressors on the job, ranging from efforts to change oneself to efforts to change what's going on in the environment.

RESOURCES

Taking the worst-case situation first, if all your circles overlap, if you are made uncomfortable by symptoms, if you have high levels of anxiety or psychosomatic reactions, if psychologically you're *hurting*—and this happens to all of us from time to time—then you need some help.

In considering resources, first I would think of a good, competent family physician, someone you can talk to, someone who knows the other resources available in the community. There are also mental-health centers and the clinics in local hospitals which are sometimes very good. If you work for an organization with good medical facilities, there may be help there. There are usually competent psychiatrists in the community and competent clinical psychologists as well, all with the training, background, and skills designed to help the individual who has this sort of emotional difficulty.

Let's go back to our three circles. If the foremost problem is with stressors, what can you do to better understand your reaction to these factors? Can you address the problem directly, talking it over with your boss or another resource in the organization, or with a specialist in the community? Can you change or avoid the situation that's become stressful for you? Are there ways of opening communication with those who may be responsible for that stressor?

If your vulnerability circle is largest, there are medications and psychotherapy, as well as the systems discussed in the last chapter. How can you better *understand* your present mood or pattern of thinking and behaving? How can you better *understand* some of its origins? If you have difficulty doing so, perhaps you feel you need additional help. Don't be reluctant to call on a competent professional.

What of context? What can you do to better understand and minimize the influence of the environmental factors which seem overwhelming? One of the most important things is to recognize clearly that the environmental situation in which you now exist is a transitory one; it's temporary. Specific family pressures, or financial pressures will all change. A recession *will* give way to a more balanced economy. Opportunity *will* again be present. Hang onto that reality.

There is not space to go into more detail about all the available resources, but keep in mind that they are available when needed, though none provide simplistic, magic answers.

CONCLUSION

I want to close on a note of reassurance. Much of the best work of this world is done by those who are somewhat compulsive and whom many would regard as "workaholics." Others are productive because of other personality characteristics or even some neurotic symptoms which would be considered unusual at best, grossly unhealthy at worst.

While not advocating unhealthy or deviant behavior, I would point out that we do tend to use our idiosyncracies in our work. Think of the very meticulous model builder, the outgoing (even exuberantly overoptimistic) salesperson, the somewhat withdrawn laboratory researcher, the chronically suspicious detective, the compulsive and humorless accountant. Such professionals do not always have these characteristics, but when they do they don't seem to interfere seriously with job performance—although they may interfere with other aspects of life.

And if Ecclesiastes was correct in writing that there is a season for all feelings and behaviors, surely there is a task of work for all of us which best unites our present personalities with even broader work responsibilities and reflection, assessment, study, and personal growth.

It is also quite possible to devote long and hard hours to one's work and to be successful while still leading a balanced existence which is emotionally satisfying and intellectually stimulating. Solid roots in constructive activity do not in themselves create an imbalance in life. Nevertheless, one should not place all of one's intellectual and emotional eggs in the basket of the world of work.

Ideally, work should be a *process* that flows through life without limits or boundaries, completely integrated with all other aspects of our existence, much as many artists and professionals and others enjoy today. Let this be our goal with a balance of stimulus and stress permeating every facet of our lives.

INDEX